NEW M

General edit

Professor of English Literature, University of Münster

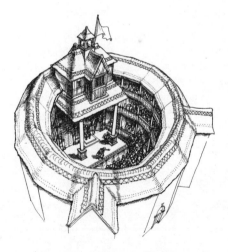

Reconstruction of an Elizabethan theatre
by C. Walter Hodges

NEW MERMAIDS

NEW MERMAIDS

THOMAS HEYWOOD

A WOMAN KILLED WITH KINDNESS

edited by Brian Scobie

University of Leeds

A & C Black • London
WW Norton • New York

First published 1985
Reprinted 1991, 1998
Reprinted with new cover 2003
A & C Black Publishers Limited
37 Soho Square
London W1D 3QZ
www.acblack.com

ISBN 0-7136-6690-0

Published in the United States of America by
W. W. Norton & Company Inc.
500 Fifth Avenue, New York, NY 10110

ISBN 0-393-90052-5

CIP catalogue records for this book are available
from the British Library and the Library of Congress

Printed in Great Britain by
Bookmarque Ltd, Croydon, Surrey

CONTENTS

INTRODUCTION

THE AUTHOR

THOMAS HEYWOOD can certainly lay claim to being the most prolific dramatist of the age of Shakespeare. His association with the theatre stretches from the mid-fifteen nineties until almost the outbreak of the Civil War in 1642. He himself tells us in the 'Address to the Reader' of *The English Traveller* that he had a hand 'or at least a main finger' in two hundred and twenty plays—and that assertion was made in 1633 when his professional career was by no means at an end. However, little is known about his life and comparatively few of the two hundred and twenty plays to which he refers can be identified today; indeed his very origins remain obscure, though he himself tells us that he is a Lincolnshire man. On the basis of that assertion and the assumption that he was of gentle rank, his biographer, A. Melville Clark, has suggested that he was the son of a Lincolnshire clergyman, Robert Heywood, Rector of Ashby-cum-Fenby and Rothwell, who had originally come from Cheshire.[1] The Rector does not appear to have been a wealthy man, but he was a scholar and may have been a graduate of the University of Cambridge. We know the dramatist spent a period in residence in Cambridge, and was something of a classicist (one of his early works was a translation of Sallust). This lends modest support to Clark's proposed identification of his family. According to the University's records Thomas Heywood would appear never to have graduated, although there are indeed a number of Thomas Heywoods mentioned in Cambridge documents for this period. One explanation may lie in the fact of the Rector's death in 1593, if he was the dramatist's father.

The first definite knowledge of Heywood comes in the business *Diary* of Philip Henslowe, the Elizabethan theatre-owner and manager. In October 1596 Henslowe made a note that he had lent to the company of the Admiral's Men thirty shillings 'for hawode's bocke'.[2] Eighteen months later, on 25 March 1598, Henslowe drew up contracts for two actors, binding them to play for him for a period of two years. One was Edward Alleyn, the other was Heywood.[3] It seems likely that this was not the

[1] See A. Melville Clark (1931), *Thomas Heywood: Playwright and Miscellanist*, pp. 1–6.
[2] See Henslowe's *Diary* ed. R. A. Foulkes and R. T. Rickert (1961), p. 50.
[3] Henslowe's *Diary, op. cit.*, p. 241.

beginning of Heywood's acting career with the Admiral's Men, but rather the formal regularisation or ratification of a relationship already existing. Heywood may already by that date have been working on the London stage as an actor (with the Admiral's Men or some other company). If so, he was but another actor turned playwright, like Shakespeare, in the tradition of 'upstart crows' declaimed against by Robert Greene.[4] He certainly continued as an actor until at least 1620, joining the Earl of Worcester's Men around 1600 (presumably on the expiry of his contract with Henslowe) and becoming one of the principal sharers or stockholders in that company, responsible for the management of the company's affairs as well as providing them with plays new and revised.

Worcester's Men became Queen Anne's Men with the accession of the Stuart King James I in 1603, and they were the only serious rivals to the pre-eminent King's Men, for whom Shakespeare wrote until 1612 or so. Heywood's association with the Worcester/Queen's Men was close and continuous for a period of twenty years. Clark has made use of Henslowe's *Diary* to calculate that between September of 1602 and the following March Heywood contributed to no less than nine plays. As Heywood himself acknowledged, much of his work for the Queen Anne's Men would have been collaborative (with dramatists such as Smith, Chettle, Dekker and Webster), but it does seem that during his twenty years with them he was the company's own professional dramatist.[5] We know from Henslowe's *Diary* that Heywood had been writing in the nineties, and we know too that at least one commentator of the time, Francis Meres, thought him in 1598 'among our best for comedy',[6] but it is his dramatic writing in the later period, of the Queen's Men, that is now central in critical interest in his work.

Queen Anne's Men, although they could claim to be the only significant rivals to the King's Men in this period, seem nevertheless to have been forever teetering on the brink of disaster.[7] As one of the senior members of the company—actor,

[4] Robert Greene, *A Groatsworth of Wit* (1952). Cited in E.K. Chambers, *William Shakespeare*, vol. II (1930), p. 188.
[5] See G. E. Bentley, *The Profession of Dramatist in Shakespeare's Time* (1971), pp. 37, 118–19.
[6] Francis Meres, *Palladis Tamia* (1598). Reprinted in G. Gregory Smith (ed.), *Elizabethan Critical Essays*, vol. II (1904), p. 320.
[7] For an account of the fortunes of the Queen Anne's Men, see G. E. Bentley, *The Jacobean and Caroline Stage*, vol. i (1941), pp. 158–75; C. J. Sisson, 'The Red Bull Company and the Importunate Widow', *Shakespeare Survey* VII (1954), pp. 57–68; and C. J. Sisson, 'Notes on Early Stuart Stage History', *M.L.R.* XXXVII (1942), pp. 25–36.

playwright and sharer—Heywood must have been greatly exercised by the economics of survival. These material circumstances within which their art was created are perhaps too readily forgotten when we attend to the achievements of dramatists like Shakespeare or Heywood, men whose roots in the theatre inhibited their possible interest in publication and in what is in a strict sense 'literature'. Heywood at least was quite explicit about his attitude to publication of plays:

> It hath been no custom in me of all other men (courteous readers) to commit my plays to the press: the reason, though some may attribute to my own insufficiency, I had rather subscribe in that to their severe censure, than be seeking to avoid the imputation of weakness, to incur a greater suspicion of honesty: for though some have used a double sale of their labours, first to the stage and after to the press, for my own part I here proclaim myself ever faithful to the first and never guilty of the last.[8]

Heywood's commitment to the theatre is here emphatic, but in spite of what has been said about the economic realities of Elizabethan and Jacobean professional drama, Heywood is not a creature of the marketplace, his conduct and morality dictated by commercial opportunism. Loyalty and honesty are the traditional presiding virtues in this passage, set as counters to dishonesty and profit.

After the collapse of the Queen's Men, Heywood's involvement with the professional London theatre seems to have been reduced. It is generally agreed that he did not act after 1620, nor does he appear to have been a sharer in any of the companies. However, he does seem to have maintained as association with Christopher Beeston, and certainly he continued to write plays, for Beeston's companies produced Heywood's plays. Between 1624 and 1634, for example, *The Captives, The English Traveller, The Fair Maid of the West, Part II*, and *A Maidenhead Well Lost* were all performed at Beeston's Phoenix by the Lady Elizabeth's Men or Queen Henrietta's Company. It is possible that Heywood was therefore working as a professional dramatist for Beeston's companies.

In the last decade of his life he exploited another market for his theatrical experience and skills. From 1630 until 1639 he provided pageants for the annual Lord Mayor's shows in seven years out of eight. In addition to this fairly profitable commission, he was increasingly turning to pamphlet publication and to prose and lengthy poems like his *Hierarchy of the Blessed Angels*. One of

---

[8] 'Address to the Reader', *The Rape of Lucrece* (1608). See also G. E. Bentley, *The Profession of Dramatist . . .*, chapter X.

the subjects to which he warmed was evidently the defence of women. He published a *History of Women* in 1624, and returned to the subject in 1640 with his *Exemplary Lives and Memorable Acts of Nine of the Most Worthy Women of the World.* His championing of women is consistent with the broadly sympathetic handling of the guilty heroine in *A Women Killed with Kindness.*[9]

Heywood died in 1641 and was buried in the church of St James in Clerkenwell on 16 August, the register describing him as 'Tho. Heywood, Poet'. What is most striking about his literary career is its range and (above all) its productivity, rather than its quality. Heywood was prepared to turn his hand to almost any form of literary production, but with an overwhelming preference for the stage. He had a keen sense of the dignity and importance of theatre, the worth of actors and acting, as his *Apology for Actors* testifies.

THE PLAY

(i) THE PLAY AND ITS CRITICS

The dramatic force of Heywood's play has always been acknowledged and admired. In particular, the three-part movement of the main plot, punctuated as it is by Anne's fall, Frankford's judgement, and the reconciliation of the couple in the final death scene, offers a powerful drama of domestic happiness undermined, overset, and destroyed, only for the mildness and restraint of the wronged husband (mild and restrained that is, by the standards of his age) to prove the means at once to Anne's death by suicide and to the re-affirmation of the Frankfords' marriage at the moment of her death. Here is material enough to create high emotion and invite stylistic indulgence, yet the plainness of Heywood's style well expresses the domestic nature of the story, and confirms its closeness to the contemporary world of the audience. The emotional intensity of the drama is not amplified but simply exposed by language which seeks to avoid high-flown rhetoric and scarcely uses figurative language at all. Lamb's remarks about Heywood being a kind of 'prose Shakespeare', suggest precisely one measure of his achievement.[10]

However, the play and its author have been subject to criticisms

---

[9] For the controversy about women see Louis B. Wright, *Middleclass Culture in Elizabethan England* (1935), and M. L. Johnson, *Images of Women in the Works of Thomas Heywood* (1975).

[10] Charles Lamb, *Speciments of English Dramatic Poets* (1808). (Notes to the selection from *A Woman Killed with Kindness*.)

which have often seemed to be iterations of the same point, though they have come in various guises. The first and most important charge concerns Heywood's 'artistry' or artistic responsibility. Almost inevitably this reveals itself as an attack upon his moral insight or even his integrity. The problematic issues are: the function of the subplot within the play; the motivation and credibility of his characters; and the absence in the play's conclusion of any moral insight or synthesis, so that tragedy is sacrificed to sentiment. T. S. Eliot, for example, deplored the subplot, defended the credibility of the character of Anne (whose fall is the test case for Heywood's handling of motivation in this play), but damned the work finally for its failure on the last count. It is worthwhile to let our discussion of the play rest upon these critical issues, for by them it is ultimately measured.

To begin therefore with the subplot. From the time of Hazlitt until the mid-twentieth century (and sometimes beyond), the Mountford-Acton underplot has invariably been derided. Usually it was seen as the product of that very prolific variety that clearly (so it was inferred) suggested that Heywood was a writer dictated to by the demands of his audience, and ultimately seduced by the temptations of commercial success. In such arguments, Heywood's artistry was vitiated by his willingness to answer the appeals of commercialism and give his audience what they cried for.[11] Yielding too readily to such vulgar (because popular) tastes meant for these critics that Heywood presented us with the image of an art flawed because it had compromised with its consumer. In the case of *A Women Killed With Kindness*, his most significant play, the damage could most clearly be seen in the pointless gesturing of the subplot, and the evident failure to unify the double plot structure. Hazlitt's comment on the management of plot in Heywood is a relatively mild anticipation of what was to follow from later critics:

> Heywood's plots have little of artifice or regularity of design to recommend them. He writes on carelessly, as it happens, and trusts to Nature, and a certain tranquility of spirit, for gaining the favour of the audience.[12]

Hazlitt was also critical of the play's conclusion, which he found both awkward and morally equivocal.

[11] As late as 1962 Arthur Brown felt the need to justify his use of the words 'art' and 'artistry' with application the Heywood. See A. Brown, 'Thomas Heywood's Dramatic Art' in *Essays on Shakespeare and the Elizabethan Drama in Honor of Hardin Craig* (1962), ed. Richard Hosley, pp. 327–39.
[12] W. Hazlitt, *Lectures in the Dramatic Literature of the Age of Elizabeth* (1818), pp. 55–60.

The attack against Heywood's supposed artlessness and care-lessness sharpened with Swinburne.[13] Whereas Hazlitt had noted with some admiration and approval Heywood's reported ability to compose a sheet a day, attributing to it in some measure the 'unembarrassed facility of his style', and remarking merely of the two hundred and more plays 'the more a man writes, the more he can write',[14] Swinburne pressed the charge of compromise. It was Swinburne too who was responsible for the commercial term made more memorable by Eliot's later use of it: 'A purveyor of this kind of ware'.[15]

When T. S. Eliot came to review A. Melville Clark's study of the playwright his language (at least) was apparently a good deal informed by that of his poetic predecessor.[16] Not only 'purveyor' and 'underplot', but Swinburne's characterisation of the dramatist as 'humble and homely' and Swinburne's adaptation of Hazlitt's 'facility', all find their way into Eliot's influential essay. Heywood was, says Eliot, 'a facile and sometimes felicitous purveyor of goods to the popular taste.'[17] The reading of Clark's book simply confirmed in large measure the gathering critical orthodoxy about Heywood. There is, it is true, a good deal more to Eliot's criticism than the mere complaint that Heywood sacrificed artistry to commercial expediency, but it is from just such a complaint that Eliot's criticism stems. And, of course, the subplot is the clearest example of his dereliction.

It is in the underplot, as in some other plays, that Heywood is least skilful. This theme—a man ready to prostitute his sister as payment for a debt of honour—is too grotesque even to horrify us; but it is too obviously there merely because an underplot is required to fill out the play for us to feel anything but boredom when it recurs. Middleton's *The Changeling*, in every other respect a far finer play, must share with *A Woman Killed With Kindness* the discredit of having the weakest underplot of any play in the whole Elizabethan repertory.[18]

Revaluation began in 1946 with an article by Freda L. Townsend entitled 'The Artistry of Thomas Heywood's Double Plots'.[19] Her choice of the word 'artistry' is a precise defiance of the traditional judgement. She classified Heywood's Double Plots

---

[13] A. C. Swinburne, *The Age of Shakespeare* (1908), pp. 197–251.
[14] Hazlitt, *op. cit.*, p. 59.
[15] Swinburne, *op. cit.*, p. 241.
[16] The review first appeared in the *TLS* for 30 July 1931, and was subsequently reprinted in *Selected Essays* (1932), pp. 171–81.
[17] T. S. Eliot, *Selected Essays*, p. 172.
[18] Eliot, *op. cit.*, p. 177.
[19] Freda L. Townsend, 'The Artistry of Thomas Heywood's Double Plots', *Philological Quarterly* 25 (1946), pp. 97–119.

into three types: (a) two plots which complement one another, or, taken together, illustrate some common theme; (b) two plots causally interrelated in a complicated story; and (c) plots that have neither causal not thematic relation to one another, but which relieve or act as a foil one to another by judicious timing of the shifts from one plot to the other. In Townsend's view *A Woman Killed With Kindness* is of the first class, that is, thematically unified. According to her, the Mountford-Acton plot illustrates the theme of honour secured only through the sacrifice of female virtue, while the Frankford-Wendoll plot proposes honour lost with female virtue. A series of contrasts then emerges between the two actions, and in particular between the two sets of characters, principally the contrast of Susan Mountford with Anne Frankford, which is seen by Townsend as the opposition between 'the rewards of virtue and the wages of sin'.[20] Similarly there are contrasts between Frankford and Acton and between Wendoll and Sir Charles, and also between the happy reconciliation of the subplot and the tragic reconciliation of the mainplot, and so on. The balance between the two plots is recognised and acknowledged as appropriate. The growth of the subplot out of the opening scene of the mainplot in such a way that the two actions only gradually become distinct, for example; the subsequent care with which the two actions remain separate, not intruding one upon the other; and likewise the conclusion of the minor action before the major one: these are evidences of care (not carelessness) that ensure the dramatic effect is one of complementary contrast and not confusion or inept 'padding'. Heywood emerges from Townsend's study with an enhanced reputation for originality, careful and conscious artistry, and integrity.

With few exceptions, criticism of Heywood in general and *A Woman Killed With Kindness* in particular has, since 1946, taken its direction from Townsend and Eliot. It would hardly be too much to say that it has been criticism of Eliot and Townsend. An important contribution was that of Peter Ure who wrote an article endorsing Townsend's claims for the thematic unity of *A Woman Killed With Kindness,* but modifying the statement of theme and directing our attention very properly back to the paradox in the play's title.[21] Both actions explore what he calls the 'burden of kindness' which is so unexpected by those who receive it as to be felt as threatening, even fatal. It is certainly helpful to be offered a

---

[20] Townsend, *op. cit.,* p. 102.
[21] Peter Ure, 'Marriage and Domestic Drama in Heywood and Ford', *English Studies* XXXII (1951), pp. 200–16.

broader reading than that implied by the contrast between the 'rewards of virtue and the wages of sin', but it hardly seems just to make parallels between the tragic burden placed on the conscience of the adulterous wife by the kindness of the offended husband and such niceties of honour as afflict Sir Charles when the hitherto cruel and malicious Sir Francis offers to relent and discharge Mountford from his debts. Parallels they do in some sense offer, but not sufficiently matched to constitute the morally instructive contrast worthy to stand at the centre of the play itself. Ure comments:

> In the conclusion, Acton's magnanimity to Susan is balanced by Frankford's passionate compassion as his wife dies. Both men have been consistently kind and these final mercies are a consumation of their Magnificence.[22]

But both men have manifestly not been consistently kind. Frankford has certainly shown generosity of spirit and action throughout the play, but Acton is a very late convert to magnanimity and kindness, and hardly impresses one as the type of Magnificence! Although Ure himself acknowledges discrepancies of other sorts between the two actions, he does not sufficiently allow for the mismatch between the two relative expressions of the theme as he describes it in plot and subplot. He does indeed suggest that the subplot offers an external and superficial expression of misfortune, as compared with the irremediably tragic misfortune that befalls the unsuspecting Frankford. Consistent with this distinction is the fact that the subplot allows (as tragic subplots can afford to allow) for a happy conclusion of its action, while the mainplot of course offers no such prospect. But Ure ultimately detects the limitations of the play in the moral ambiguities of the endings to both plots, which for him are neither fully explored nor adequately justified. Since he reads Kindness as itself proposing the central thematic paradox, experienced as a 'monstrous' moral burden by the characters to whom it is extended, it is for him less than satisfactory that the response of those characters should be (to say the least) so negative—that is, that the best reply the play can make is to offer suicide as a morally appropriate resolution.

The main plot does present us with a dramatisation of the moral paradox that Kindness can prove destructive—whether we look for this paradox in the consequences of the kindness Frankford extends to Wendoll (which is a generosity of spirit seeking to share benefits and pleasures with others less fortunately endowed

[22] Ure, *op. cit.*, p. 204.

than himself), or in the kindness that expresses itself as restraint and control when the discovery of Anne's infidelity provokes him to wrath and vengeance (which is mercy). Such generosity and mercy are divine in character; such weakness and fallibility as provokes them are sadly human. Here indeed may lie the seeds of a tragic theme. But in the subplot neither is the Kindness with which we have to deal of this order (it is in fact long overdue), nor is the recipient so much morally burdened by it as he feels himself disadvantaged in honour, in a narrow sense socially burdened. Emulation is the mode within which the characters of the subplot function, almost to the last. Kindness finally consists for them in laying that mode aside, but it shows itself too late in the secondary action to constitute an appropriate thematic explanation and justification of that action. And, in any case, Kindness here is provoked by romantic Love—love at first sight—and is therefore creative rather than destructive in its consequences. Kindness felt as a moral burden is then never quite appropriate as a description of the subplot, which seems to reach in quite other directions.

The French critic, Michel Grivelet, claims much for Heywood's careful artistry and thematic unity. His 1957 study of Heywood certainly takes the defence of *A Woman Killed With Kindness* further.[23] The burden of his case is that the unity of the play is conscious and complex. He describes it as being threefold: (1) above all, unity of theme; (2) a productive symmetry existing between the plots; and (3) the direct connections existing between plot and subplot in terms of character and situations. An important contribution which Grivelet makes to our sense of the complex unity of the play is the attention he gives to Heywood's exploitation of the complexity and ambiguity of language as a means of asserting the unity of the play. It is an amplification of Ure's observations about the thematic significance of Kindness to be reminded that the word bore for the Renaissance its own richness, of which Hamlet's play on words—'A little more than kin and less than kind'—is for the subplot at any rate an appropriate hint. The use of the word 'match' in the play is vitally instructive in the way it serves to link plot and subplot in the opening scene, proposing on the one hand harmony and perfect concord, and on the other opposition, emulation and conflict. The double use of the word in these opening exchanges at the marriage celebrations is itself unsettling—and anticipatory of much that follows. Heywood picks up the word again at the moment when the newly alerted and suspicious Frankford attempts to read his fate in the language of the card-games, and in the process finds himself initiated into a world of *double entendre* and shifting meanings. The untrustworthiness of language in this scene makes explicit for Frankford an irony, or at any rate an ironic possibility, in language which had simply by other means been suggested to the audience who witnessed in the first scene one 'match' swiftly give way to another. It might also be observed that the matched hands of the marriage ceremony are, of course, re-joined in the final scene, and that out of a match with hawks and hounds and the bitter enmity that ensues, is ultimately made a match between Susan and Sir Francis Acton.

Grivelet makes another important contribution to our understanding of the complex unity of the play when he recalls Bescou's remarks that the house itself is one of the principal characters in the play.[24] In so far as this may be said to be true of both plots, it is instructive to compare the two actions in this respect, for in the distinction a good deal is revealed about Heywood's use of the double plot and his thematic complexity. In the main plot, as Grivelet notes, the house has a kind of spiritual presence in the drama—'La maison est troublée et se tourmente en ceux qui l'habite'.[25] Frankford's return in the night, stealing like a thief through his own house with false keys, is a subversion of domestic order. Like the marriage, the house is itself violated. The notion of domestic sanctity is well attested by his words as he enumerates the keys:

> But this, the door that's bawd unto my shame,
> Fountain and spring of all my bleeding thoughts,
> Where the most hallowed order and true knot
> Of nuptial sanctity hath been profaned.
> It leads to my polluted bedchamber,
> Once my terrestrial heaven, now my earth's hell,
> The place where sins in all their ripeness dwell—(XIII, 8-16)

The identification of the house with his marriage, with his earthly happiness and all that he values most, his domestic Eden, makes Anne's banishment from it inevitable. That all traces of the disappointed promise of paradise should be sent with her is also understandable when we remember the ethos within which the hero of his age was schooled. The symbolic irony of the lute and its reminder of past harmony, literal and figurative, makes clear the sense of loss that dominates Frankford's reaction.[26]

[24] Grivelet, *op. cit.*, p. 212.
[25] Grivelet, *op. cit.*, p. 212.
[26] See Cecile W. Cary, 'Go Break this Lute: Music in Thomas Heywood's *A Woman Killed with Kindness*', *Huntington Library Quarterly* 37 (1974), pp. 111-22.

When we turn from middle-class marriage to the affairs of Sir Charles and his sister, Susan, we máy say likewise that the house is of great importance in their world. It seems at times also the very cornerstone of their values, identical in large measure with their sense of honour. When we first encounter Sir Charles at the marriage feast he is not without a kind of arrogant pride in his financial means. His attitude to the wager with Sir Francis is almost defensively extravagant, irresponsibly willing to put at risk large sums as though a carelessness with money testified to his social status, his honour. When in time he is deprived of financial means and compelled to labour what is revealed is what he thinks of as the true source of his nobility: he remains a gentleman by virtue of his ability to cling to the house and estate that was the origin of his family's gentility. It is worth noting that he will consider the surrender of Susan, but not of the house! What this tells us is that the code of honour to which Sir Charles subscribes, though it is again symbolically represented by the house, differs significantly from Frankford's sense of domestic sanctity of home and marriage. Instead, the notion of 'house' held dear by Sir Charles is identical with honour in the family name, with lineage which both establishes identity and asserts gentility. What is thematically significant is the interrelation between these two allied but distinct senses of 'house'.

Here is a clue to the kind of unity Heywood gave his play, a unity in which the subplot makes a vital contribution to the texture of language and ideas at work within the play as a whole, because it offers perspective and context for the action of the main plot, paralleling situations and characters, and playing variations on ideas and language. The difficulty is to articulate the theme in a way that acknowledges this rich complexity (which incidentally so defies the old orthodox view of Heywood's 'simplicity'). As we have said, chastity is too narrow an expression by far of what the play is about. Charity is a far better definition of what lies ultimately at the centre of Heywood's concern, but while the play may be ultimately concerned with Charity or Kindness or Mercy, it is not only taken up with these essentially Christian values but also with competing or complementary sources of value and relative claims. In the subplot, for example, while conflict may be resolved through the agency of romantic love, the play is for the most part an action driven by chivalrous values of reputation, gentility, and aristocratic pride, as we have said, medieval in character and social in preoccupation; they contrast sharply with the domestic and bourgeois values discovered by Frankford in his marriage. In Scene IV, Frankford sees marital contentment as the cornerstone of earthly happiness, not fame nor worldly reputation nor birth nor social standing nor wealth (though these values have their adherents elsewhere in the play). The tragically fragile nature of worldly happines is confirmed even here where it seems most modest, and the main plot must thereafter seek to reconcile the affirmation of value in domestic marital contentment with the moral law. It is achieved through invoking what has been present throughout the play—the scheme of divine love, forgiveness and mercy of which human love is the imitation. For a Christian audience the ending provides a satisfactory conclusion, because in it human love discovers its own nature, the powers it possesses which link it with the divine act of love. Guilt, repentance and atonement assert the Christian message. Frankford's assumption of the role of the Redeemer is almost sacriligious.[27] Although the direct typological parallels are not evident in the affairs of Acton and Mountford, yet there too it is love that ransoms all ill deeds, a form of romantic love consistent with the key in which the subplot is mainly played. Yet, of course, some details of the ending are worryingly unorthodox. The most glaring instance is the confident way in which Anne contemplates salvation in spite of the fact that she has been guilty of two cardinal sins—adultery and suicide. Forgiveness, mercy, charity, or kindness prevail, but neither its occasions nor its consequences are ever simple, given the nature of man, fallen and fallible. Hence the paradox of the title. Not only Kindness in the simple sense, but kinship seems to be part of this extended exploration of human values. From kin we expect kindness; kindness is kinship, whether relative or absolute. In the subplot kin prove conspicuously unkind. In her quest for help from those bound to her and her brother by ties of kinship and past kindness, Susan Mountford meets nothing but unkind replies. Here is grotesque burlesque of Sir Charles's faith in the external fact of his house as assurance of his gentility:

If this were sold, our names should then be quite
Razed from the bead-roll of gentility (VII. 36-7)

and Susan reports that 'our kindred with our plenty died' (X. 70).This cynically materialist definition of kinship as a denial of kindness is represented also in Shafton, the unscrupulous confirmation of Old Mountford's view that 'This is no world in which to pity men,' and Tydy's 'each man for himself!' (IX. 5 &

---

[27] For another reading of the analogy between Frankford and Christ see John Canuteson, 'The Theme of Forgiveness in the Plot and Subplot of *A Woman Killed with Kindness*', *Renaissance Drama* (n.s.) 2 (1969), pp. 123–47. Canuteson's criticism is discussed briefly below, pp. xxv–xxvi.

34). Shafton offers specious 'kindness' with malicious and opportunist intent. Between Shafton's acquisitive greed and Sir Charle's 'wrested courtesy' Heywood brings into focus within the scope of the subplot the older, medieval, chivalric values associated with the Court and the aristocracy (with their code of honour), and, on the other hand, the new, acquisitive, materialist values of the mercantile classes. These modes of behaviour and exhibitions of value provide the social and moral perspectives for the central issue of the domestic tragedy. In the subplot the spirit of emulation, bitter rivalry and competition dominates. Against such a climate the moment of resolution stands in sharp contrast by the fact of its disinterestedness, by no longer seeking advantage. Emulation has been expressed through the finite and accountable tokens of the usurer, whether he may have dealt directly in money or property or in the more ideal balance-sheet that measures the debts and credits of honour. All are in the end replaced by the redemptive infinity of Love. In this way we may understand the conventional and short-hand resolution of Acton's romantic conversion, which otherwise must seem psychologically inept and dramatically uninventive and trite.

In the main plot the unaccountable mystery of Kindness, Charity or Love (call it how we will) is put to a sterner trial. Frankford's manifest generosity is tested by the betrayal of the fallible Anne and the ungrateful Wendoll, and yet survives to become at once the instrument of moral law (compelling Anne not only to acknowledge her own guilt but to choose her own punishment) and the means of redemption. At the same time as the tragedy is made realistic and domestic, the Christian reference is increasingly felt.

(ii) GENRE AND CHARACTERISATION

A reading of the play that finds it essentially Christian (as our reading here has) should surprise no one. There is good evidence to confirm that Heywood himself regarded the drama as a didactic medium well suited to the propagation of virtue and the condemnation of vice. His pamphlet defence of the theatre, *An Apology for Actors*, was published in 1612, and in it he argues very strongly indeed in favour of the beneficial effects of drama so far as justice and morality in society are concerned. As we shall see, at least one of the illustrations he makes use of seems pertinent to *A Woman Killed With Kindness*.

In the three books of *An Apology for Actors*, Heywood attests to the antiquity, dignity and true uses of the drama. The most prominent argument is that of moral utility—that the theatre contributes largely to the moral improvement of audiences by bringing before them instances of virtue and vice to be emulated or abhorred accordingly. A defence of drama based upon emphasising its didactic character was, of course, quite unexceptional in the period, for most theoretical discussions of literature or art at that time stressed the moral nature of their effects upon the audience or reader. In doing so the apologists were doing no more than replying in kind to their detractors, whose hostility invariably took the form of a puritan concern with moral effects.

Heywood suggests that such contribution as the drama offers to social well-being might take on a political complexion, for the exposure of tyranny on the stage might serve as a warning to would-be despots.

> Am I Melpomese, the buskined muse
> That held in awe the tyrants of the world,
> And played their lives in public theatres,
> Making them fear to sin, since fearless I
> Prepared to write their lives in crimson ink
> And act their shames in eye of all the world?[28]

Alternatively, the drama might take the direction defined by the Morality tradition and be directed to the exposure of sins and crimes. The drama could besides offer its audience models of heroic behaviour in action before their eyes. Heroic action represented on the stage might indeed, Heywood interestingly suggests, be a yet more effective model if the subjects were taken from what he calls 'our domestic histories':

> To turn to our domestic histories, what English blood seeing the person of any bold Englishman presented doth not hug his fame and hunny at his valour . . . it hath power to new mould the hearts of the spectators and fashion them to the shape of any noble attempt.[29]

Heywood argues that the didactic function of the theatre is undeniable, for in all ages it has been thought that dramatic action 'was the nearest way to plant understanding in the hearts of the ignorant.'[30]

In the third book of his *Apology* he distinguishes the ways in which the various genres or sub-genres within the drama fulfil this function. Tragedies, he tells us, are presented in order to 'terrify men from the like abhorred practices'. Histories either

[28] *An Apology for Actors*, f. B2r.
[29] *op. cit.*, f. B4r.

work by 'animating men to noble attempts, or attaching the consciences of the spectators, finding themselves touched in presenting the vices of others'. Foreign instances are applied to the vices and virtues of contemporary Englishmen. Morality plays, he claims, act to 'persuade men to humanity and good life, to instruct them in civility and good manners, showing them the fruits of honesty and the end of villainy'.

> Briefly, there is neither Tragedy, History, Comedy, Moral or Pastoral from which an infinite use cannot be gathered.[20]

Of particular relevance to the present text is the assertion that through the agency of plays

> The unchaste are by us shown their errors, in the persons of Phrine, Lais, Thais, Flora: and amongst us, Rosamund, and Mistress Shore. What can sooner print modesty in the souls of the wanton than by disovering unto them the monstrousness of their sin?[32]

And to clinch this point Heywood relates the tale of a Norfolk woman who was so affected by the staging of the 'old history of Friar Francis' in which a young wife murders her husband in order to secure the affections of her lover that the woman confessed spontaneously to a similar crime some seven years previously. This instance of the play's ability to catch the conscience of the spectator occurred, according to Heywood, 'within these few years'. In the light of such evidence, Hamlet's hopes for *The Murder of Gonzago* are by no means extravagant.

There is in the *Apology* no explicit suggestion that Heywood thought domestic plays, such as *A Woman Killed With Kindness*, dealing directly with the lives of contemporary English men and women, would serve the didactic purposes by which he justifies drama any more effectively. But there are hints that such might be the case in his remarks upon Histories, and in the fact that Heywood found 'domestic and home-born truths' to be the burden of the most extravagant or remote action.

A Woman Killed With Kindness is often included in the sub-genre known as Domestic Tragedy, a dramatic type supposedly established by *Arden of Faversham* (1592). Heywood's *English Traveller* provides another example of what he could achieve in this vein. Domestic Tragedy has been defined by H. H. Adams in his *English Domestic or Homiletic Tragedy* (1943), principally in terms of the social rank of its main characters, who stand 'below

---

[30] *op. cit.*, f. F4r.
[32] *op. cit.*, f. G1r.

the ranks of nobility,' but also in terms of the homiletic purposes it seeks to serve, attempting to inculcate moral lessons on a Christian nature by locating the action in a world familiar to the audience and tracing in it the tragic consequence of sin or immorality. According to Adams, the domestic tragedies exhibit strongly the homiletic pattern of passion leading to crime, discovery, repentance, temporal punishment, and the hope of eternal mercy and ultimate salvation.[33] The extent of the presence and influence of the homiletic tradition upon these domestic plays is, however, a controversial point. Madeleine Doran, for example, maintained in her *Endeavors of Art* (1953) that the domestic tragedies were far from being the 'dramatized sermons' that Adams proposed. The didactic intention in Heywood's play is less prominent than Adams suggests since the ethical point of view from which the action is regarded 'moves harmoniously with the fable'.[34] Moreover, *A Woman Killed With Kindness* differs from many if not all of the plays written within the domestic tragedy type by not being a dramatisation of contemporary historical events, as were *Arden* and most of the plays that followed it. In other words, Heywood's work answers less to the demands either of didactic or topical interest than was usual within the sub-genre, although it is true that it shares with Adams' tragedies the domestic emphasis and the middle-class setting. It is certainly possible to discover the homiletic pattern within the plot, but we may justifiably doubt that Heywood set out with the didactic intention of moulding his events to that pattern. Heywood was conscious of offering his audience something distinctive in subject, theme and style, as the Prologue shows. He was not offering his audience a dramatized version of recent bloody and sensational events. The story is not, as *Arden* is, for example, a tale of murder. And it is the tragic events, the sympathetic involvement with the characters, that claim our attention, not the revelation of a homiletic pattern. Doran's judgement in this respect is just. In the final phase, Heywood contrives that the form of punishment hit upon by Frankford be at once more merciful (and therefore more Christian) and at the same time more intense in its moral assertion through being self-inflicted. Frankford's kindness not only sears the conscience of his wife, but thereby compels her to accept responsibility for punishing her own deeds. Choosing her own punishment, she confirms the truth of the moral judgement as she understands it. Acknowledgement points

---

[33] See H. H. Adams, *English Domestic or Homiletic Tragedy, 1575–1642* (1943), *passim*.
[34] M. Doran, *Endeavors of Art* (1953), p. 351.

the way to salvation, or the possibility of salvation, through action that affirms without imposing a moral code. She completes the affirmation rather. As such, it seems a subtle development of the homiletic pattern; perhaps it would be juster to say a development from the pattern. What Heywood's play achieves, if judged by the definition offered by Adams, far transcends Adams' limits. Just as it served no purpose to think of *A Woman Killed With Kindness* as an artless concession to popular tastes, neither should we conceive of it as a prim sermon on homiletic lines.

Are Heywood's characters mere conventional ciphers? Apparently not, for they have provided some considerable difficulties of interpretation. The most frequently noted problem is that of Anne's fall, which hardly seems provided with adequate motivation. But more recently Frankford's motives have also exercised critical ingenuity, and a good deal of quarrelling has centred on precisely what his paradoxical kindness amounts to. Speculation has been born of the absence of clear motives for Anne's behaviour and of the ambiguity of Frankford's paradoxical punishment. Increasingly the superficially obvious interpretation—that Anne is a sinner exemplifying the traditional belief in the fallibility of womankind, and that Frankford is a Christian gentleman whose kind treatment of his erring wife fulfills an impeccable religious injunction (while at the same time proving ultimately more effective than the expected responses of the cuckolded husband)—has been challenged, even to the point where Anne is accorded the status of heroine while her husband is described as 'despicable'. Such a turn-around in critical thinking demands attention.

Patricia M. Spacks provides a useful starting-point for consideration of such 'modern' criticism.[35] She begins indeed by saying that no one has attempted a modern reading that defends the play against the customary charges of improbability and weak characterisation. Appeals to convention and traditional attitude are appeals to what is largely an outmoded, historical understanding of the play. Her contention is that the play can be seen to speak directly to the present, 'an age more disillusioned than its own'. The unity that Spacks discovers in the play derives from the extent to which appearances are deceptive. The most obvious case is Anne Frankford, whose perfection crumbles at the first temptation. Wendoll is another whose appearance proves misleading. Frankford is the man deceived in both cases though we are encouraged to see him as an honourable man. His goodness is

[35] Patricia M. Spacks, 'Honor and Perception in *A Woman Killed with Kindness*', *M.L.Q.* XX (1959), pp. 321–32.

frustrated by the fact that he does not perceive clearly. In the subplot, Patricia Spacks finds further evidence of perversity of vision. Kinship goes unacknowledged or denied, friendships prove false, honour is 'wrested' to the point where (in Spacks' view, at least) property takes precedence over Susan's virginity and the Mountfords seem to propose satisfying their debt by delivering Susan's corpse to Acton! Acton, although he has proved a malicious villain since the opening scene, gains the romantic reward of the woman he desires at the end, and is even permitted the moral advantage of commenting adversely upon Wendoll. As Spacks concludes, though the endings may satisfy convention and sentiment, they hardly bear scrutiny from a strictly moral point of view.

> Of the five principal characters in the play who demonstrate in more or less subtle ways failures of honour, only one, Mistress Frankford, is punished—for she is the only one who fully recognises and repents her own failure ... The world of *A Woman Killed With Kindness* is not a world of true and significant moral standards—it is rather a world of appearance. The appearance of honour is accepted as a substitute for the real thing; the appearance of prosperity makes men kinsmen; the appearance of virtue is enough to insure a happy ending. The only major character who does conform to a true and rigid vision of honour, Master Frankford, is himself trapped in the world of appearances to the extent that he is unable to perceive and judge truly.[36]

Spacks finds the spokesman for moral normalcy in Nick, the servant, whose role therefore underlines the moral irony of the world of the play. In this and in other respects it is a valuable reading of the play. What it mostly suggests is that if we were to deprive the play of its conventional structures we would find ourselves with a very different, less comforting work, certainly an unsentimental one. Moreover, the dichotomy between appearance and reality serves to generalise the tragedy and thereby avoid the (historically defended) suggestions of Bescou, Hardin Craig and Hallett Smith that it is in the fact of Anne's femininity that we ought to find the explanation of her weakness and the source of the tragedy. In Spacks' reading all prove fallible in their judgements and perceptions. Human fallibility, not female frailty, is Heywood's subject.

It is difficult (especially in the latter half of the twentieth century) to remain silent in the face of a text that appears to treat women at best with patronising sympathy, while it places them firmly within a world dominated by men. This is revealed jestingly in those remarks at the wedding celebrations about

[36] Spacks, *op. cit.*, p. 330.

taking a wife down in her wedding shoes, but more sinisterly in
the way that both Anne Frankford and Susan Mountford are
offered up almost as sacrificial victims to the value-systems
obtaining in the play. I do not think that it can quite be said of
this play as it can, I think, be said of *The Changeling,* for example,
that the heroine is corrupted precisely because she finds herself a
token in a masculine world, made conscious of the empire of
masculine proprietorial values that prove instrumental upon her
very moral responses. Yet Anne, who barely acts except submis-
sively, enjoys more of our sympathies than Beatrice-Joanna who
strives (benightedly to be sure) in order to control her own
destiny. She is never a willing sinner, and never seems in any real
doubt as to what course she would follow were she allowed any
real choice. Why is her choice (for, of course, she has one) not a
'real choice'? Her plea to Frankford not to ride out on the fatal
night of her discovery seems altogether genuine. Can nothing be
said on behalf of such a gentle, unwilling sinner?

   In an interesting article entitled '*A Woman Killed with
Kindness:* An Unshakespearian Tragedy' David Cook, like Eliot
before him, finds the scene of Anne's fall perfectly credible, and
the reason he finds it so credible differs from Eliot's by its appeal
to the shaky foundation of the Frankford marriage.[37] Anne is
defenceless before an empassioned assault upon her emotions
because the marriage has not engaged her emotionally—hers is no
more than a 'calmly affectionate marriage'. Wendoll makes a
simple statement of his passion; he does not behave with the
sophistry of a villain. Any doubts we may entertain about the
apparent cynicism of his final remarks (which for most readers are
precisely what distinguish him from Anne) are explained by Cook
as self-mocking irony. As for Frankford and his wife:

> The simple conception of Frankford as a long-suffering and unequivocally
> virtuous man, and of Anne as the utterly vicious, sinning wife, seems to me the
> major limitation in most critiques of the play . . . [It] is to over-simplify the play,
> to miss much of its serious investigation of the characters, and, indeed, to fail to
> recognise the tragic irony of the title.[38]

In Cook's view the tragedy is a tragedy of inadequacy, and the
inadequacy is that of John Frankford, who 'will never have any
conception of the powerful force which impelled Anne into
adultery' and who 'has no awareness of his own insufficiency'.
Cook finds him not only inadequate in his relationship with

[37] David Cook, '*A Woman Killed with Kindness:* An Unshakespearian Tragedy',
English Studies XLV (1964), pp. 353–72.
[38] Cook, *op. cit.,* p. 360.

Anne, but also cold, deliberately setting out to torment her soul, as the text itself allows. As compared by Cook with Wendoll, Frankford begins to take on the role of villain of the piece:

> In all this he is contrasted with Wendoll . . . who acts wrongly but feels aright; Frankford acts properly but denies his feeling. As Wendoll suffers at the last by facing his actions and feelings honestly, Frankford suffers by running away and hiding behind inflexible morality.
>
> It is Frankford's realisation of his own wrongness which makes the final packed climax of the play.[39]

Comparison of the plots also suggests to Cook a contrast between Frankford (who sacrifices neither life nor moral self-importance) and Sir Charles Mountford (who risks all in a bold proposal to his sister). Of the discovery scene he says, 'There is nothing mean or small about [Anne's] sin, as there is about [Frankford's] virtue.' For him, 'Anne's calibre exceeds Frankford's throughout.'[40] The weaknesses in their marriage that leave it vulnerable are the result of the wife's inexperience and the absence of passion in the relationship. It is a calm and affectionate, but a complacent partnership, and for this the fault is Frankford's, according to Cook (though we might ask why the burden of providing more falls upon him exclusively). When Anne succumbs to temptation, Frankford's response is consistent with his limitations as Cook has already suggested them—he cannot comprehend why she has done such a thing, and he is cold in his punishment. Coldness and complacency are to Cook greater sins than illicit passion and adultery.

> Anne Frankford touches pitch, but is not defiled. She acts wrongly, but never (like Frankford) coldly. She finds Wendoll's passion irresistibly returned by her own feelings, but this passion does not harden or qualify her quiet love for Frankford. Nor is she complacent; she is terribly aware of the impossible duality of feeling within her: experience does not deaden her sensibilities; she is no Beatrice-Joanna.[41]

It is not so much complacency and coldness that John Canuteson finds to complain of in Frankford, rather a subtle cruelty that the critic finds 'despicable'.[42] It is the absence of forgiveness that for Canuteson characterises Frankford's behaviour as cruel, unacceptable and ultimately unchristian. His implication is that Anne is naively trapped within the limits of her

[39] Cook, *op. cit.*, p. 362.
[40] Cook, *op. cit.*, p. 365.
[41] Cook, *op. cit.*, p. 366.
[42] Canuteson, *op. cit.*

husband's perverted theology, whereby the path to her salvation lies through his forgiveness.

> My fault so heinous is
> That if you in this world forgive it not,
> Heaven will not clear it in the world to come. (XIII. 86–8)

Canuteson seems to me here both right and wrong. A glance at St Paul, a general understanding of theological teachings on the subject of marriage in the seventeenth century, or a reading of Milton should be enough to assure us that Anne's emotionally correct, dramatically appropriate (or at least understandable) feelings about the need for Frankford's forgiveness had after all some basis in orthodox belief, however deplorable we might find them now.

Margaret B. Bryan offers the final instance of these recent revisionary attempts upon the play. In her article 'Food Symbolism in *A Woman Killed With Kindness*',[43] she claims Frankford as a neurotic, a repressed homosexual whose invitations to Wendoll to 'use my table' are unconscious expressions of sexual desire, since eating symbolizes lust in Heywood's play (having indeed a well-based traditional association between them—evident in literature and apparently confirmed by science). The absence of any eating in the early marriage scene she thinks a deliberate omission that prognosticates what she calls the Frankfords' 'unhappy marriage'.[44] It follows neatly that the form of suicide chosen by Anne is starvation. Bryan's attack upon Frankford includes the accusation that he never in the course of the play makes what Bryan calls 'a sincere avowal of his love to Anne.'[45] And she perversely complains that when he lists those things that make his life a happy one he puts her at the end of the list! On the other hand, she detects in him the 'pathological need to be cuckolded',[46] a purpose he blindly and unconciously pursues, but which reveals itself in an investigation of the images and symbolic usages of food and eating in the play. The suggestion that modern psychology enables one to see Frankford as offering his wife to Wendoll provides another link between plot and subplot—for does not Sir Charles offer his sister to Acton in a parallel way?

There is much to admire in Margaret Bryan's study of food symbolism. It certainly provides another indication of the

---

[43] M. B. Bryan, 'Food Symbolism in *A Woman Killed with Kindness*' *Renaissance Papers* (Duke Univ., N.C. 1974), pp. 9–17.
[44] Bryan, *op. cit.*, p. 15.
[45] Bryan, *op. cit.*, p. 14.
[46] Bryan, *op. cit.*, p. 15.

thematic and imaginative unity of the play, even if we find her conclusions at odds with the dictates of commonsense. It is worth remembering that the only expressions of reservation spoken when Frankford extends his invitation to Wendoll are spoken by Anne herself:

> As far as modesty may well extend,
> It is my duty to receive your friend. (IV. 81-2)

But to find Frankford neurotic, or despicable, or cold and complacent, and thereby to implicate him in the tragedy is to seek to rationalize the events. It is to squirm against the fact that tragedy teaches us nothing but empathy. Which, after all, is everything.

NOTE ON THE TEXT

There are two early authoritative editions of this play. One is the Quarto of 1607, the other the Quarto of 1617, which describes itself on the title-page as the 'third Edition'. There are good reasons for assuming that the 1607 Quarto is in fact the First Edition of the play, and no reasons at all for challenging the statement that the 1617 Quarto is the Third Edition. It therefore appears that a Second Edition was produced sometime between 1607 and 1617, but is now no longer extant. However, this missing edition may have a bearing upon the relationship between Q1 (1607) and Q3 (1617) and their respective claims to textual authority.[1]

The First Quarto exists in a unique copy now in the British Library. The title-page reads:

A/ WOMAN/ KILDE/ with Kindneſſe./ *Written by Tho: Heywood.*/ [device: McKerrow 355]/ LONDON/ Printed by William Iaggard dwelling in Barbican, and/ are to be ſold in Paules Church-yard./ by Iohn Hodgets. 1607.

It is gathered A–H⁴ [–A1] and consists of 31 unnumbered leaves, having the title on A2 recto, the Prologue on A3 recto, and the text beginning on A4 recto.

It is also certain that the copy for Q1 was authorial manuscruipt rather than theatrical prompt book. There are a number of reasons for this view. In the first place, the 1607 quarto reveals some uncertainty about the name of Sir Charles's sister. When she first appears she is 'Iane' (scene III) before Heywood settles for 'Susan' (with a vestigal 'Iane' in Scene XIV). There are also the imprecise stage directions referring to '*3. or 4. seruingmen*' (Scene VIII), '*countrie Wenches, and two or three Musitians*' (Scene II), or the entry of an unspecified number of '*Seruingmen*' (twice in Scene XII). There is some confusion over the number of persons killed in the quarrel scene between Sir Charles and Sir Francis. The stage direction indicates that '*one of Sir Francis his huntsmen*' is killed, but Charles is immediately repentant and wishes to 'breathe in them new life, whom I have slain.' He is discovered by his sister 'among the dead' and taken by the Sheriff to answer for the lives 'of these dead men.' Vagueness and indecision of this kind we would expect to find only in copy very close to authorial

---

[1] The fullest analysis of the play's printing history is given by K. M. Sturgess, 'The Early Quartos of Heywood's *A woman killed with kindness*' in *The Library* (5th series) xxv (1979), pp. 93–104.

foul papers; it would certainly not be tolerated in any theatrical manuscript. It is also reasonable to expect that any reprinted edition of the play would have made some attempt to eliminate the inconsistencies at least, and for this reason it seems likely that the quarto of 1607 is indeed the First Edition, even though the absence of any entry in the Stationers Register makes the dating of the first publication less than absolutely sure.

There are, moreover, indications that the spelling and punctuation of the 1607 quarto correspond with Heywood's in the manuscript of *The Captives* and *Callisto*.[2] Sturgess suggests that we can see characters develop in Heywood's foul papers, citing the example of Spiggot, emerging from the Butler of earlier scenes as late as Scene XII. Or Sisly, who has no independent existence in the stage entry for scene II (being merely one of the 'Wenches'), but who becomes a significant minor character as Anne's serving-maid. There is much to confirm the belief that authorial foul papers provided the copy for Q1.

The second authoritative edition extant is the quarto of 1617 which describes itself on the title-page as the 'Third edition'. The transcription is as follows:

A/ WOMAN/ KILDE/ with Kindneſſe./ *As it hath beene oftentimes Acted by/ the Queenes Maiest. Seruants./ Written by* THO. HEYWOOD./ The Third Edition./ {device: McKerrow 283)/ LONDON,/ Printed by Iſaac Iaggard, 1617.

The book consists of 36 leaves, A–I⁴, regularly signed \$3, and having the title-page on A1 recto, the Prologue on A2 recto, and the Text from A3 recto to I4 recto, with an Epilogue on the verso of the final leaf. No press variants have been reported, nor have I found any. One bibliographical fact of interest to emerge, however, is that the compositor who appears single-handedly to have set this edition was almost certainly Jaggard's compositor B, whose working practices have been pretty well investigated and recorded in view of his influence upon the printing of Shakespeare's texts in particular.[3]

The central issue of Q3's relationship to Q1 turns upon the question of the copy text for the 1617 quarto. The two scholars who have hitherto given closest scrutiny to the early quartos, R. W. Van Fossen and K. M. Sturgess, reach quite different

---

[2] See K. Palmer's review of Van Fossen's edition in *M.L.R.* lvii (1962), p. 415.
[3] Sturgess cites D. F. MacKenzie, 'Compositor B's role in *The Merchant of Venice*, Q2 (1619)', *SB* xii (1959), pp. 75–90. Also Alice Walker, *Textual Problems in the First Folio* (1953) and 'Compositor Determination and Other Problems in Shakespearean Texts; *SB* vii (1955), pp. 3–15; and W. S. Kable, 'Compositor B, the Pavier quartos and copy spellings; *SB* (1968), pp. 129–61.

conclusions. Van Fossen frankly admitted that he was unable to determine the relationship between the two editions, but was at least prepared to state that there were no bibliographical links between them that were capable of demonstration. He argued for the independent authority of Q3 on the grounds of a series of distinctions between the two editions, each of which has been carefully contraverted by Sturgess: (a) Q3 is (unusually for a reprint) longer than Q1. (Attributable almost entirely, says Sturgess, to a change in type-size.) (b) Q3's spellings and speechheads do not show the influence of Q1. (Sturgess reminds us that it is precisely compositor B's marked spelling and typographical habits that identify his work.) (c) Van Fossen claims that there are marked differences in lineation between the two quartos. (Sturgess again appeals to B's known practice.) (d) There are discrepancies between the two in the marking of exits. (Sturgess explains these discrepancies as resulting from *ad hoc* editing by the compositor, accounting in this way for all but one omission in Q3.) Van Fossen's conclusion that Q1 and Q3 derive independently from manuscript or manuscripts is clearly shaken by Sturgess's explanations. The latter goes on to argue that the copy for Q3 was not a revised manuscript, but probably a copy of Q2 (in its turn derived bibliographically from Q1), which had at some stage in its descent been subject to revision.

Having disarmed Van Fossen's argument for the independence of the two extant editions, Sturgess presents his evidence for the presence of Q1-derived copy in Q3. The 'strong bibliographical link' and 'short line of descent' are supported by the following arguments: (a) An explanation of textual confusion in Scene III, lines 25–30, and a similar textual misreading in Scene VII, line 40. (b) The omission of a speech-head in both quartos at Scene III, line 57. (c) Indications that the substitution of lower case for upper case 'w' in Q1 led to a similar substitution in Q3. (d) The suggestion that lineation differences show B's 'characteristically cavalier treatment of copy-text,' assuming his copy to have been Q1.

A number of these arguments deserve closer attention. Sturgess give no reference for the third point and it is therefore hard to take it seriously. There are many instances of lower case for upper case 'w' in Q3, in italic at least. The instance that he mentions (Scene XI, line 45) is plausibly explained by the influence of Q1, through there is already some evidence of desperation on the part of the compositor to find cap. W at this stage of his setting.

Sturgess's second argument regarding the omission of the speech-heading for Susan/Jane does *not* stand up to examination. The omission of the character's name when she speaks immediately following her entry is, as he says, unique in Q1. Unfortunately, it is not so rare in Q3. Sturgess claims that there is but one other instance (an exception which he explains away as the consequence of the compositor having already a full measure). I have counted five instances in Q3 of an entry followed by a speech unsignalled by a speech-head. The arrangement is far from uncommon in Q3 when a character enters alone and immediately speaks. Its bibliographical significance is minimal (see Susan in Scene III; Shafton in Scene V; Wendoll in Scene VI; Shafton in Scene VII; and Wendoll in Scene XVI).

If we turn now to the first argument in favour of linking Q1 to Q3 bibliographically, we enter the area of textual criticism. On two occasions Q1, according to Sturgess, was responsible for misreadings which Q3 unsuccessfully attempted to correct, demonstrating its dependence by its failures. The first of these two instances occurs in the argument between Sir Francis and Sir Charles in Scene III. In Q1 two successive speeches are assigned to Sir Francis, quite erroneously. The correction proposed by Q3 gives the second speech to Charles, alters the next two speech ascriptions accordingly before suppressing one speech-head and running two speeches from Q1 together in order to restore the pattern of speakers as in the 1607 quarto. Sturgess maintains that in so doing the compositor of Q3 (or Q2) misunderstood the nature of the mistake, which was a simple omission of the speech-heading from the final line of what appears as the first of the successive speeches attributed to Sir Francis. The alternatives may be clarified as follows:

1607	1617	Sturg.	Text
Fran.	Fran.	Fran.	...she did discomfit Some of her feathers, but she brake away!
		Char.	Come, come, your hawk is but a rifler.
Fran.	Char.	Fran.	How?
Char.	Fran.	Char.	Ay, and you dogs are trindle-tails and curs.
Fran.	Char.	Fran.	You stir my blood!
Char.		Char.	You keep not one good hound in all your kennel, Nor one good hawk upon your perch.

Sturgess's emendation is attractive not least because it is economical in its explanation of the original fault. It is also made apparently more plausible by the observation that the line from which Q1 dropped the speech-head ('Come, come, your hawk is but a rifler.') begins a new page (B3 recto) in Q1. In effect, this means that the error of the dropped speech head occurred not once but twice, since the catchword reads 'Come,' when we would expect *'Char.'* The likelihood of the compositor making an error with a word which he had to set twice is presumably somewhat diminished. But the question also arises of the effect upon the text of any such change as Sturgess proposes. Sturgess himself allows that Sir Charles's guilt is increased by his emendation, while the changes in the 1617 text 'obscure' that guilt. The line in question is either an insulting riposte to Sir Francis's rationalization of the match, or it is the culmination of that same defence. Of the two characters, it is Sir Francis who subsequently reveals himself as the more cruel and malicious, and (by contrast) Sir Charles who enjoys our sympathies. The rash insults directed against hawks and hounds are perhaps for that reason more likely to come from Francis. He has also in the circumstances more cause to be heated than Charles. It may also be thought doubtful that a man whose language has risen to the choler of 'rifler' and 'trindle-tails and curs' would then descend to the plainness of 'You keep not one good hound in all your kennel,/Nor one good hawk upon your perch.' In this respect it must be said that the Q3 emended text makes quite as much sense as that proposed by Sturgess, and offers no real inconsistencies, in spite of inferring rather more confusion in the papers which provided copy-text for Q1. I have therefore retained the Q3 reading in the present text.

The second instance of textual 'corruption' concerns a word in Scene VII, line 40, when Sir Charles is describing the hardship he and his sister have endured to retain their land.

> This palm you see
> Labour hath glowed within; her silver brow,
> That never tasted a rough winter's blast
> Without a mask or fan, doth with a grace
> Defy cold winter and his storms outface.

The Q1 text reads 'Labor hath gloud within', which becomes 'Labour hath glow'd within' in Q3, ignoring the possibility that Q1 intended 'gloved'. Sturgess proposes 'galled' and cites another Heywoodian portrait of Labour 'with galled hands'.[4] Heywood's handwriting was, of course, notoriously bad,[5] but one again there

[4] *Pleasant Dialogues and Dramas* (1637) contains the following lines in the story of Timon: 'O wondrous! Poverty by him fast stands/And the rough fellow Labor, with gallid hands.' (Cited by Sturgess, p. 102.)

[5] See W. W. Greg's *English Literary Autographs 1550–1650* (1925) and *Dramatic Documents from the Elizabethan Playhouses* (1931), and the Malone Society reprint of *The Captives* (1953) for specimens.

is nothing inconsistent about the quarto readings, and I have favoured a conservative reading of this line, adopting Q3's 'glowed'. In other words, I have not accepted that Q1 was a misreading (merely a spelling variant) nor that Q3 offers an erroneous emendation. Consequently, the proof of further linkage between Q1 and Q3 is not here established.

Having consistently challenged the basis of Sturgess's case for Q3's dependence on Q1, we are brought to a position which seems barely an advance upon Van Fossen's disavowal. The strength of Sturgess's confidence that Q3 depended upon the earlier printed edition seems misplaced, although he has certainly established it as something more than a possibility. The text for this edition is based upon Q1 as the only clearly authoritative edition. Very few of the variants supplied by Q3 are not attributable to compositorial intervention. Instances of revision that require more than an alert compositor would normally supply include the correction of inconsistency over Susan/Jane and at Scene XVII, line 55 the change from 'maister Frankford' to 'brother Acton'. It may be that such faults in Q1 were sufficiently serious to merit the author's attention in preparing copy for the second or third editions. The case in favour of the dependence of Q3 on Q1 remains the stronger, and can easily accommodate a theory of authorial revision in these few instances.

ABBREVIATIONS AND REFERENCES

Q1	*A Woman Kilde with Kindness* (1607)
Q3	*A Woman Kilde with Kindness (1617)*, 'The third Edition'
Baskervill	*Elizabethan and Stuart Plays*, edited by C. R. Baskervill, V. V. Heltzel, and A. H. Nethercot (1934)
Bates	*A Woman Killed with Kindness and The Fair Maid of the West* edited by K. L. Bates, (1917)
Chappell	*Old English Popular Music*, edited by W. Chappell, and revised by H. E. Wooldridge (1893)
Dodsley	*Select Collection of Old Plays*, vol, iv, edited by James Dodsley (1744)
E.S.	*Essays and Studies*
M.L.Q.	*Modern Language Quarterly*
M.L.R.	*Modern Language Review*
N.&Q.	*Notes & Queries*
OED	*Oxford English Dictionary*
Tilley	*A Dictionary of the Proverbs in England in the Sixteenth and Seventeenth Centuries*, edited by M. P. Tilley (1950)
Van Fossen	*A Woman Killed with Kindness*, edited by R. W. Van Fossen (1961)
Verity	*Thomas Heywood*, edited by A. W. Verity (1888)

FURTHER READING

H.H. Adams, *English Domestic or Homiletic Tragedy 1575 to 1642* (1943).

David Atkinson, 'Review Article (of present edition)', *Cahiers Elisabethains* 30 (1986), pp. 117–23.

David Atkinson, 'An approach to the main plot of Thomas Heywood's *A Woman Killed with Kindness*', *English Studies* 70 (1989), pp. 15–27.

F. S. Boas, *Thomas Heywood* (1950).

Rick Bowers, '*A Woman Killed with Kindness:* Plausibility on a Smaller Scale', *SEL* 24 (1984), pp. 293–306.

L. Brodwin, *Elizabethan Love Tragedy 1587–1625* (1971), pp. 101–21

Laura B. Bromley, 'Domestic Conduct in *A Woman Killed with Kindness*', *SEL* 26 (1986), pp. 259–76

Arthur Brown, 'Thomas Heywood's Dramatic Art, in *Essays on Shakespeare and the Elizabethan Drama in Honor of Hardin Craig*, ed. Richard Hosley (Columbia, Missouri, 1962), pp. 327–40.

M. B. Bryan, 'Food Symbolism in *A Woman Killed with Kindness*', *Renaissance Papers* (Duke Univ., N.C., 1974), pp. 9–17.

John Canuteson 'The Theme of Forgiveness in the Plot and Subplot of *A Woman Killed with Kindness*', *Renaissance Drama* (new series) 2 (1969), pp. 123–47.

Cecile W. Cary, ' "Go breake This Lute": Music in Heywood's *A Woman Killed with Kindness*', *Huntington Library Quarterly* 37 (1974), pp. 111–22.

A. Melville Clark, *Thomas Heywood: Playwright and Miscellanist (1931)*.

David Cook, '*A Woman Killed with Kindness:* An Unshakespearian Tragedy', *English Studies* XLV (1964), pp. 353–72.

Herbert R. Coursen, 'The Subplot of *A Woman Killed with Kindness*', *English Language Notes* II (1965), pp. 180–85.

Hardin Craig, *The Enchanted Glass: the Elizabethan Mind in Literature* (1936).

O. Cromwell, *Thomas Heywood: a Study in the Elizabethan Drama of Everyday Life* (1928)

T.S. Eliot, 'Thomas Heywood', *TLS*, 30 July 1931. Reprinted in *Selected Essays* (1932), and *Elizabethan Essays* (1934).

Harry Garlick, 'Anne Frankford's Fall: A Complementary Perspective', *AUMLA* 61 (1984), pp. 20–28.

Michel Grivelet, 'The Simplicity of Thomas Heywood', *Shakespeare Survey* XIV (1961), pp. 56–65.

Michel Grivelet, *Thomas Heywood et le Drame Domestique Elizabéthan* (1957).

Nancy A. Gutierrez, 'The Irresolution of Melodrama: The Meaning of Adultery in *A Woman Killed with Kindness*', *Exemplaria* I (1989), pp. 265–91.

William Hazlitt, *Lectures on the Dramatic Literature of the Age of Elizabeth* (1818).

Diana C. Henderson, 'Many Mansions: Reconstructing *A Woman Killed with Kindness*', *SEL* 26 (1986), pp. 277–94.

George C. Herndl, *The High Design: English Renaissance Tragedy and the Natural Law* (1970), pp. 168–83.

G. Hooper, 'A Woman Killed with Kindness, Scene xiv: Sir Charles's Plan', *English Language Notes* Xl (1974), pp. 181–8.

———

Lisa Hopkins, an article on *A Woman Killed with Kindness*, *Connotations*, 1994–5

Diana Henderson, 'A Woman Killed with Kindness: a response to Lisa Hopkins', *Connotations*, 1995–6, 50–54.

Michael Wentworth, 'A Woman Killed with Kindness and the genetics of genre formation – a response to Lisa Hopkins', *Connotations*, 1995–6, 55–68.

S. J. Wiseman, 'More on reading domestic tragedy and A Woman Killed with Kindness – another response to Lisa Hopkins', *Connotations*, 1996–7, 86–91.

Lisa Hopkins, 'A Woman Killed with Kindness – an author's response', *Connotations*, 1996–7, 92–94.

———

M.L. Johnson, *Images of Women in the Works of Thomas Heywood* (1975). Salzburg Studies in English Literature series.

Frederick Kiefer, 'Heywood as Moralist in *A Woman Killed with Kindness*', in *Medieval and Renaissance Drama in England* 3 (1986), pp. 83–98.

Paula McQuade,'"A Labyrinth of Sin": Marriage and Moral Capacity in Thomas Heywood's *A Woman Killed with Kindness*' *Modern Philology*, Vol. 98, no. 2 (2000), pp. 231–50.

Irving Ribner, *Jacobean Tragedy* (1962), pp . 50–71.

Hallet D. Smith, 'A Woman Killed with Kindness', *PMLA* 53 (1938), pp. 138–47.

Patricia M. Spacks, 'Honor and Perception in *A Woman Killed with Kindness*', *M.L.Q.* XX (1959), pp. 321–32.

K. M. Sturgess, 'The Early Quartos of Heywood's *A woman killed with kindness*', *The Library* (fifth series) XXV (1970), pp. 93-104.

K. M. Sturgess (ed.), *Three Elizabethan Domestic Tragedies* (1969).

A.C. Swinburne, *The Age of Shakespeare* (1908).

Freda L. Townsend, 'The Artistry of Thomas Heywood's Double Plots', *Philological Quarterly* 25 (1946), pp. 97–119.

Peter Ure, 'Marriage and the Domestic Drama in Heywood and Ford', *English Studies* XXXII (1951), pp. 200–16.

R. W. Van Fossen (ed.), *A Woman Killed with Kindness* (1961). Revels Plays series.

Michael Wentworth, 'Thomas Heywood's *A Woman Killed with Kindness* as Domestic Morality', in *Traditions and Innovations*, eds D. B. Smith and R. A. White (Univ. of Delaware Press, 1990), pp. 150–62.

Louis B. Wright, 'The Male Friendship Cult in Thomas Heywood's Plays', *M.L.N.* XLII (1927), pp. 510–14.

Louis B. Wright, *Middleclass Culture in Elizabethan England* (1935).

A

WOMAN

KILDE

with Kindnesse.

Written by Tho: Heywood.

PRV
DEN
TIA

LONDON

Printed by William Iaggard dwelling in Barbican, and
are to be sold in Paules Church-yard,
by Iohn Hodges. 1607.

[DRAMATIS PERSONAE

JOHN FRANKFORD
ANNE FRANKFORD, *his wife, sister of Sir Francis Acton*
WENDOLL, *friend of Frankford*
SIR CHARLES MOUNTFORD
SUSAN MOUNTFORD, *his sister*
SIR FRANCIS ACTON
CRANWELL, *friend of Frankford*
MALBY, *friend of Sir Francis*
OLD MOUNTFORD, *uncle of Sir Charles*
TYDY, *cousin of Sir Charles*
SANDY, *former friend of Sir Charles*
RODER, *former tenant of Sir Charles*
SHAFTON, *false friend of Sir Charles*
NICK, *servant of Frankford*
JENKIN, *servant of Frankford*
SPIGGOT, *Frankford's butler*
SISLY MILK-PAIL, *servingwoman to Frankford*
ROGER BRICKBAT ⎱ *country fellows, Frankford's farm servants*
JACK SLIME ⎰
JOAN MINIVER ⎱
JANE TRUBKIN ⎰ *country wenches, Frankford's farm servants*
ISBEL MOTLEY ⎰
SHERIFF
KEEPER
SERGEANT
MUSICIANS, HUNTSMEN, FALCONERS, SERVINGMEN, SERVING WOMEN, CARTERS, COACHMAN, FRANKFORD'S CHILDREN, OFFICERS]

3

THE PROLOGUE

I come but like a harbinger, being sent
To tell you what these preparations mean:
Look for no glorious state, our muse is bent
Upon a barren subject, a bare scene.
We could afford this twig a timber tree,   5
Whose strength might boldly on your favours build;
Our russet, tissue; drone, a honey-bee;
Our barren plot, a large and spacious field;
Our coarse fare, banquets; our thin water, wine;
Our brook, a sea; our bat's eyes, eagle's sight;   10
Our poet's dull and earthy muse, divine;
Our ravens, doves; our crow's black feathers, white.
  But gentle thoughts when they may give the foil,
  Save them that yield, and spare where they may spoil.

---

1 *like* Q1 (as Q3)
5 *afford* put forward, present
7 *our russet, tissue i.e.* that our plain clothes were fine
13 *gentle* of gentlemen, and women. A reflection upon the implied social status and breeding of the audience
13 *give the foil* bring about the overthrow or defeat. The term comes from wrestling (*OED*), where it signifies something less than a *fall*.
14 *spoil* destroy

Cf Shakespeare's Prologue to *Henry V*

4

SCENE I

Enter MASTER JOHN FRANKFORD, SIR FRANCIS ACTON, MISTRESS
ANNE FRANKFORD, SIR CHARLES MOUNTFORD, MASTER MALBY,
MASTER WENDOLL, *and* MASTER CRANWELL

SIR FRANCIS
Some music there! None lead the bride a dance?

SIR CHARLES
Yes, would she dance 'The Shaking of the Sheets'.
But that's the dance her husband means to lead her.

WENDOLL
That's not the dance that every man must dance
According to the ballad.

SIR FRANCIS   Music ho!   5
By your leave, sister—by your husband's leave
I should have said—the hand that but this day
Was given you in the church, I'll borrow. Sound,
This marriage music hoists me from the ground.

FRANKFORD
Aye, you may caper, you are light and free.   10
Marriage hath yoked my heels, pray then pardon me.

SIR FRANCIS
I'll have you dance too, brother.

SIR CHARLES   Master Frankford,
You are a happy man, sir, and much joy
Succeed your marriage mirth. You have a wife
So qualified, and with such ornaments   15
Both of the mind and body. First, her birth
Is noble, and her education such
As might become the daughter of a prince,
Her own tongue speaks all tongues, and her own hand

---

2 *The Shaking of the Sheets* a popular ballad tune, here referred to with a bawdy
double entendre. In the ballad the dance is that of the dying (see Wendoll's remark
in 1.4), which in its turn strikes an appropriately ominous note in the play,
anticipating Frankford's 'A cold grave must be our nuptial bed.' (Scene XVII, 124)
5 *according to the ballad* See the note on line 2. The relevant lines from the ballad are
    Can you dance the shaking of the sheets,
    A dance that every man must do?
See Chappell, I, 228
11 *pray then pardon me* Q1 (pray pardon me Q3)

---

5 *Music Ho!* For the thematic significance of music in the play see Cecile W. Cary
'"Go Break Thus Lute": Music in Heywood's *A Woman Killed with Kindness*',
Huntington Library Quarterly, 37 (1974), pp. 111–122

Can teach all strings to speak in their best grace, 20
From the shrill treble, to the hoarsest base.
To end her many praises in one word,
She's beauty and perfection's eldest daughter,
Only found by yours, though many a heart hath sought
    her.

FRANKFORD

But that I know your virtues and chaste thoughts, 25
I should be jealous of your praise, Sir Charles.

CRANWELL

He speaks no more than you approve.

MALBY

Nor flatters he that gives to her her due.

ANNE

I would your praise could find a fitter theme
Than my imperfect beauty to speak on; 30
Such as they be, if they my husband please,
They suffice me now I am married.
His sweet content is like a flattering glass,
To make my face seem fairer to mine eye,
But the least wrinkle from his stormy brow, 35
Will blast the roses in my cheeks that grow.

SIR FRANCIS

A perfect wife already, meek and patient.
How strangely the word 'husband' fits your mouth,
Not married three hours since, sister. 'Tis good;
You that begin betimes thus, must needs prove 40
Pliant and duteous in your husband's love.
Godamercies, brother, wrought her to it already?
'Sweet husband,' and a courtesy the first day?
Mark this, mark this, you that are bachelors,
And never took the grace of honest man, 45
Mark this against you marry, this one phrase:

---

21 *shrill* Q1 (shrill'st Q3)
27 *approve* show to be true (by marrying her)
36 *blast* wither, blight, shrivel
42 *Godamercies* Q1 (Gramercies Q3)
43 *courtesy* curtsy, a gesture of submission
45 *took the grace of honest man* i.e. married, became husband
46 *against* 'in anticipation of the time when' (Van Fossen)

'In a good time that man both wins and woos
That takes his wife down in her wedding shoes.'

FRANKFORD
Your sister takes not after you, Sir Francis.
All his wild blood your father spent on you;   50
He got her in his age when he grew civil.
All his mad tricks were to his land entailed,
And you are heir to all. Your sister, she
Hath to her dower her mother's modesty.

SIR CHARLES
Lord sir, in what a happy state live you;   55
This morning, which to many seems a burden
Too heavy to bear, is unto you a pleasure.
This lady is no clog, as many are.
She doth become you like a well-made suit
In which the tailor hath used all his art,   60
Not like a thick coat of unseasoned frieze,
Forced on your back in summer. She's no chain
To tie your neck, and curb you to the yoke,
But she's a chain of gold to adorn your neck.
You both adore each other, and your hands   65
Methinks are matches. There's equality
In this fair combination; you are both scholars,
Both young, both being descended nobly:
There's music in this sympathy; it carries
Consort and expectation of much joy,   70
Which God bestow on you, from this first day
Until your dissolution—that's for aye.

---

48 *takes... shoes* asserts superiority over her from the first day of their marriage. The
   phrase appears to be proverbial, though not in *Tilley* or the *Oxford Dictionary of
   Proverbs*. Van Fossen cites an instance in Dekker

50 *spent on you* used engendering you, and therefore bequeathed you. Sir Francis's
   actions in the play would tend to confirm that he has inherited his father's rashness,
   as here suggested by Frankford

51 *civil* decent, sober, responsible

52 *to his land entailed* bestowed inseparably with the land; who inherited the one,
   inherited the other

54 *dower* dowry

58 *clog* an impediment attached to the heels or necks of prisoners to prevent escape, a
   block of wood, here used figuratively

61 *unseasoned frieze* a thick coarse woollen cloth, worn out of season

63 *curb* Q3 (curbs Q1)

65 *adore* Q1 (adorne Q3)

69 *sympathy* harmony, concord

70 *consort* accord, agreement, concurrence

:IS

ep you here too long, good brother Frankford.
        le hall! Away, go cheer your guests!
What, bride and bridegroom both withdrawn at once?   75
If you be missed, the guests will doubt their welcome
And charge you with unkindness!

FRANKFORD   To prevent it,
I'll leave you here, to see the dance within.

ANNE
And so will I.

SIR FRANCIS   To part you it were sin.

                    [*Exeunt* FRANKFORD *and* ANNE]

Now gallants, while the town musicians   80
Finger their frets within, and the mad lads
And country lasses, every mother's child
With nose-gays and bride-laces in their hats,
Dance all their country measures, rounds and jigs,
What shall we do? Hark, they are all on the hoigh;   85
They toil like mill-horses, and turn as round,
Marry, not on the toe. Ay, and they caper,
But without cutting. You shall see tomorrow
The hall floor pecked and dinted like a millstone,
Made with their high shoes; though their skill be small,   90
Yet they tread heavy where their hobnails fall.

SIR CHARLES
Well, leave them to their sports. Sir Francis Acton,
I'll make a match with you: meet me tomorrow
At Chevy Chase, I'll fly my hawk with yours.

SIR FRANCIS
For what? for what?

SIR CHARLES   Why, for a hundred pound.   95

---

83 *bride-laces* laces of gold silk formerly used to tie nosegays in the hats of wedding
guests. 'A nosegay bound with laces in his hat, bridelaces, sir' cited in *OED* from
Porter's *Angry Woman of Abingdon* (1599)

85 *on the hoigh* eager, excited

86 *turn as round* the horse driving a mill turned only by plodding round in a circle

88 *cutting OED* records that to cut in dancing was to 'spring from the ground, and
while in the air to twiddle the feet one in front of the other alternatively, with great
rapidity.' The first instance of this sense is given from Florio in 1603

93 *me* Q1 (*omitted* Q3)

94 *Chevy Chase* the placename is apparently derived from the ballad of that name,
which gives an account of a famous border skirmish

SIR FRANCIS
Pawn me some gold of that.

SIR CHARLES   Here are ten angels,
I'll make them good a hundred pound tomorrow
Upon my hawk's wing.

SIR FRANCIS   'Tis a match, 'tis done.
Another hundred pound upon your dogs,
Dare you Sir Charles?

SIR CHARLES   I dare. Were I sure to lose,   100

I durst do more than that: here's my hand,
The first course for a hundred pound.

SIR FRANCIS   A match.

WENDOLL
Ten angels on Sir Francis Acton's hawk;
As much upon his dogs.

CRANWELL
I am for Sir Charles Mountford, I have seen   105
His hawk and dog both tried. What, clap you hands?
Or is't no bargain?

WENDOLL   Yes, and stake them down,
Were they five hundred they were all my own.

SIR FRANCIS
Be stirring early with the lark tomorrow.
I'll rise into my saddle ere the sun   110
Rise from his bed.

SIR CHARLES   If there you miss me, say
I am no gentleman: I'll hold my day.

SIR FRANCIS
It holds on all sides. Come, tonight let's dance;
Early tomorrow let's prepare to ride.
We had need be three hours up before the bride.   115

[*Exeunt*]

96 *Pawn* deposit as security for the wager, pledge
96 *angels* a gold coin
102 *course* race or competition between two hounds after game
106 *clap* shake (to seal the wager)
107 *stake them down* deposit as a pledge in the wager
112 *hold my day* keep my appointment

SCENE II

Enter NICK *and* JENKIN, JACK SLIME, ROGER BRICKBAT *with*
COUNTRY WENCHES [*including* SISLY MILK-PAIL], *and* TWO *or*
THREE MUSICIANS

JENKIN
Come Nick, take you Joan Miniver to trace withall; Jack
Slime, traverse you with Sisly Milk-pail. I will take Jane
Trubkin, and Roger Brickbat shall have Isbel Motley,
and now that they are busy in the parlour, come, strike
up, we'll have a crash here in the yard.   5

NICK
My humour is not compendious: dancing I possess not,
though I can foot it; yet since I am fallen into the hands of
Sisly Milk-pail, I assent.

JACK SLIME
Truly Nick, though we were never brought up like
serving courtiers, yet we have been brought up with   10
serving creatures, ay and God's creatures too, for we have
been brought up to serve sheep, oxen, horses and hogs,
and such like. And though we be but country fellows, it
may be in the way of dancing, we can do the horse-trick as
well as servingmen.   15

1 *trace* dance
2 *traverse* 'to march up and down, or to move the feet with proportion, as in dancing'
   Bullokar *An English Expositor* (1616)
5 *crash* a bout of revelry, amusement
6 *humour* temperament
6 *compendious* presumably an error for "comprehensive"
8 *assent* Q1 (consent Q3)
9–10 *like serving courtiers i.e.* like gentlemen
10–11 *with serving creatures* to feed and tend the livestock, playing alliteratively on
   creature/courtier
12 *horses and hogs* Q1 (Horses, Hogges Q3)

s.d. TWO *or* THREE MUSICIANS An evidence of authorial foul papers as copy for Q1,
since such vagueness would not normally be characteristic of any manuscript used
in the playhouse
13–14 *country fellows... horse-trick* It is difficult to ignore the possibility of unconscious bawdry here, or indeed a deliberate play on words. The term *servant* was a
courtly term for a lover, and has also (in addition to the sense of *domestic attendant*)
a frankly sexual application. There is also a likely pun on horse/whores. The
passage as a whole is a defence of the farm labourers against the more 'courtly'
household servants

ROGER BRICKBAT
  Ay, and the cross-point too.

JENKIN
  O Slime, O Brickbat! Do not you know that comparisons
  are odious? Now we are odious ourselves too, therefore
  there are no comparisons to be made betwixt us.

NICK
  I am sudden and not superfluous;   20
  I am quarrelsome, and not seditious;
  I am peaceable, and not contentious;
  I am brief, and not compendious.
  Slime, foot it quickly. If the music overcome not my
  melancholy I shall quarrel, and if they suddenly do not   25
  strike up, I shall presently strike thee down.

JENKIN
  No quarrelling for God's sake: truly, if you do, I shall set a
  knave between you.

JACK SLIME
  I come to dance, not to quarrel. Come, what shall it be?
  'Rogero'?   30

JENKIN
  'Rogero'? No, we will dance 'The Beginning of the
  World'.

16 *cross-point* a dance step, but also with bawdy possibilities
18 *odious* presumably he means 'we too are servants, inferiors' but with a play on
   odorous, glancing at the intimacy of Slime with his sheep, oxen, horses and hogs
20 *sudden* peremptory, prompt
20 *superfluous* inclined to do more than is necessary
21 *seditious* turbulent, causing trouble
29 Q1 reads *'Slime. I come...'* without an indented speech-head, perhaps the speech
   makes one very full line
31 *'Rogero'* A popular tune
31–2 *'The Beginning of the World'* An alternative name for 'Sellenger's Round', another
   popular tune

---

23 *compendious* Nick would appear to be carried away by the flow of his own rhetoric.
   This word of course means 'brief' with the sense of economical, succinct, concise.
   How he might conceive of it as a demerit is not clear. See above (line 6) where his
   misunderstanding of the word is again assumed
24 *Slime, foot it* Q1 (*Slime. Foot it* Q3—as though it were a new speech attributed to
   Slime) The confusion in Q3 comes from the setting of Q1 which sets lines 20–23 as
   verse, and then begins a prose line with this phrase. Q1 does not however indent
   'Slime' as is its practice with speech-heads

SISLY
I love no dance so well as 'John, Come Kiss Me Now'.

NICK
I, that have ere now deserved a cushion, call for 'The
Cushion Dance'.   35

ROGER BRICKBAT
For my part, I like nothing so well as 'Tom Tyler'.

JENKIN
No, we'll have 'The Hunting of the Fox'.

JACK SLIME
'The Hay', 'The Hay', there's nothing like 'The Hay'.

NICK
I have said, I do say, and I will say again—

JENKIN
Every man agree to have it as Nick says.   40

ALL
Content.

NICK
It hath been, it now is, and it shall be—

SISLY
What Master Nichlas, what?

NICK
'Put on Your Smock a Monday'.

JENKIN
So the dance will come cleanly off. Come, for God's sake   45
agree of something! If you like not that, put it to the
musicians or let me speak for all, and we'll have
'Sellenger's Round'.

ALL
That! that! that!

---

33 *'John...Now'* Another popular tune of the day
34–5 *'The Cushion Dance'* This dance is described in *The Dancing Master* (1703)
36 ROGER Q3 (Rogero Q1)
   'Tom Tyler' Again a tune, possibly 'Tom Tinker'
37 *'The Hunting of the Fox'* A tune so far unidentified
38 *'The Hay'* Described in C.J. Sharp's *Country Dance Book* II, 41–8, this was a
   physical and noisy country dance
39 *I have...again* Q1 (It hath bene, it now is, and it shall be Q3)
44 *'Put on Your Smock a Monday'* A popular tune, also known as 'Pretty Nancy'.
   Given in *Chappell*, I, 234
   Smock a woman's undergarment, a shift or chemise
48 *Sellenger's Round* Name of another popular tune. See *Chappell*, I, 256

NICK
  No, I am resolved thus it shall be,   50
  First take hands, then take you to your heels.

JENKIN
  Why, would you have us run away?

NICK
  No, but I would have you shake your heels.
  Music, strike up!

They dance. NICK, *dancing, speaks stately and scurvily, the rest after
          the country fashion*

JENKIN
  Hey, lively my lasses, here's a turn for thee.   55

                                        Exeunt

SCENE III

Wind horns. Enter SIR CHARLES, SIR FRANCIS, MALBY, CRANWELL,
          WENDOLL, FALCONERS, *and* HUNTSMEN

SIR CHARLES
  So! well cast off. Aloft, aloft! well flown!
  O now she takes her at the souse, and strikes her
  Down to the earth, like a swift thunderclap.

WENDOLL
  She hath struck ten angels out of my way.

SIR FRANCIS
  A hundred pound from me.

SIR CHARLES   What, falconer!   5

FALCONER
  At hand, sir.

54 s.d. *scurvily* rudely, discourteously

  s.d. *Wind* sound, blow
  FALCONERS ed. (Falconer Q1, Q3)
  2 *at the souse* as the prey was rising from the ground
  2–3 These lines are punctuated as prose in both quartos, without initial capitalisation
      in line 3

SIR CHARLES
Now she hath seized the fowl, and 'gins to plume her,
Rebeck her not, rather stand still and check her.
So! seize her gets, her jesses, and her bells.
Away!   10

SIR FRANCIS
My hawk killed too.

SIR CHARLES   Ay, but 'twas at the querre,
Not at the mount, like mine.

SIR FRANCIS   Judgement, my masters!

CRANWELL
Yours missed her at the ferre.

WENDOLL
Ay, but our merlin first hath plumed the fowl,
And twice renewed her from the river too.   15
Her bells, Sir Francis, had not both one weight,
Nor was one semitune above the other.
Methinks these Milan bells do sound too full,
And spoil the mounting of your hawk.

SIR CHARLES   'Tis lost.

7–8 As prose in Q3

8 *rebeck* beckon back, recall. This is the only example of this meaning cited in the *OED*

8 *check* Bates' emendation, adopted by Van Fossen, to the word 'cherk' makes good sense. *OED*, citing *The Book of St Albans* gives for 'cherk' or 'chirk' the meaning 'to incite by "chirking"' or making a birdlike sound with the lips. Such a reading would supply the necessary contrast with the sense of 'rebeck'

9 *gets, her jesses and her bells* The jesses were usually leather straps attached to the hawk's legs, as were the bells. 'Gets' are almost certainly the same as jesses, since they etymologically derive from the same source. They are so defined by the *OED*, giving this passage as the sole instance

11–12 *the querre ... mount* i.e. before the prey rose from the ground, not as it was rising. (See Van Fossen and Bates for a correction of the *OED* definition of 'querre')

13 *ferre* An obscure falconry term indicating one side or the other of a river. *The Book of St Albans* distinguishes between the 'fer Jutty' (the far side) and the 'Jutty ferry' (the near side). Such a distinction hardly clarifies the present usage

14 *merlin* a species of falcon, 'one of the smallest, but one of the boldest, of European birds of prey' *OED*
   hath Q1 (had Q3)

15 *renewed* drove out by attack

17 *one semitune above the other* a hawk's bells, according to *The Book of St Albans*, ought to be so pitched

18 *Milan* the metal work of this city was famous

SIR FRANCIS
    I grant it not. Mine likewise seized a fowl   20
    Within her talents, and you saw her paws
    Full of the feathers; both her petty singles
    And her long singles gripped her more than other;
    The terrials of her legs were stained with blood—
    Not of the fowl only she did discomfit   25
    Some of her feathers, but she brake away!
    Come, come, your hawk is but a rifler.

SIR CHARLES   How?

SIR FRANCIS
    Ay, and your dogs are trindle-tails and curs.

SIR CHARLES
    You stir my blood!
    You keep not a good hound in all your kennel,   30
    Nor one good hawk upon your perch.

SIR FRANCIS   How, knight?

SIR CHARLES
    So, knight? You will not swagger, sir?

SIR FRANCIS
    Why, say I did?

SIR CHARLES
    Why sir, I say you would gain as much by swaggering
    As you have got by wagers on your dogs.   35
    You will come short in all things.

22–3 *petty... long singles* short and long claws of the hawk
24 *terrials* OED thinks this an error for some term in falconry, most likely 'terrets',
    rings enabling the jesses to be attached to the leash
24–6 *with blood... away i.e.* our hawk drew blood, not just feathers, but the prey
    escaped
27 *rifler* a hawk that fails to take the prey cleanly, but seizes only feathers (*The Book of
    St Albans*)
28 *trindle-tails* dogs with curly tails, low-bred dogs
30 *a* Q1 (one Q3)
32 *swagger* quarrel, bluster, be insolent
34–6 Printed as prose in the quartos

27–31 *Come, come...perch* See K. M. Sturgess, 'The Early Quartos of Heywood's *A
    woman killed with kindness*', in *The Library* (fifth series), vol. XXV, 2 (1970), pp.
    93–104, together with the discussion in the Note on the Text, above. Sturgess
    attributes line 27 to Sir Charles, enabling him otherwise to follow Q1 in speech
    ascriptions, arguing that the 1617 edition made an unsuccessful attempt to correct
    the slip in Q1, thereby showing its dependence on the 1607 text, as well as setting
    more textual difficulties. For a detailed discussion resisting Sturgess see pp.
    xxxi–xxxii above

SIR FRANCIS   Not in this!
  Now I'll strike home!
SIR CHARLES   Thou shalt to thy long home.
  Or I will want my will!
SIR FRANCIS
  All they that love Sir Francis follow me.
SIR CHARLES
  All that affect Sir Charles draw on my part.   40
CRANWELL
  On this side heaves my hand.
WENDOLL   Here goes my heart.
                      They divide themselves

SIR CHARLES, CRANWELL, FALCONER, *and* HUNTSMAN *fight against*
SIR FRANCIS, WENDOLL, *his* FALCONER, *and* HUNTSMAN, *and* SIR
CHARLES *hath the better, and beats them away, killing both of Sir*
                    Francis his men.
              [Exeunt all except SIR CHARLES]

SIR CHARLES
  My God! what have I done? what have I done?
  My rage hath plunged into a sea of blood
  In which my soul lies drowned, poor innocent
  For whom we are to answer. Well, 'tis done,   45
  And I remain the victor. A great conquest,
  When I would give this right hand, nay, this head,
  To breathe in them new life whom I have slain.
  Forgive me God, 'twas in the heat of blood,
  And anger quite removes me from myself: 50
  It was not I, but rage, did this vile murder;
  Yet I, and not my rage, must answer it.
  Sir Francis Acton, he is fled the field,
  With him all those that did partake his quarrel,
  And I am left alone, with sorrow dumb,   55
  And in my height of conquest, overcome.
                  Enter SUSAN

37 *long home* grave (proverbial, from the Bible)
41 s.d. *Killing both* Q3 (*killing one* Q1). See Note on the Text, p. xxviii
41 *men* Q3 (*huntsmen* Q1). One of those he kills is the Falconer
56 s.d. SUSAN Q3 (*Iane* Q1). See the Note on the Text, p. xxviii

44 *innocent* Q1 (innocents Q3). The Q3 variant implies that the innocents are those he
   has killed; the word might just as easily apply to his soul, for whom he has to
   answer on the Judgement Day, and about whose drowning he is after all expressing
   concern before any remorse about the literal death of Sir Francis's men

SUSAN
O God, my brother wounded among the dead!
Unhappy jest that in such earnest ends.
The rumour of this fear stretched to my ears,
And I am come to know if you be wounded.   60

SIR CHARLES
O sister, sister, wounded at the heart.

SUSAN
My God forbid!

SIR CHARLES
In doing that thing which he forbade,
I am wounded, sister.

SUSAN   I hope not at the heart.

SIR CHARLES
Yes, at the heart.

SUSAN   O God! a surgeon there!   65

SIR CHARLES
Call me a surgeon, sister, for my soul;
The sin of murder it hath pierced my heart,
And made a wide wound there, but for these scratches,
They are nothing, nothing.

SUSAN   Charles, what have you done?
Sir Francis hath great friends, and will pursue you   ´70
Unto the utmost danger of the law.

SIR CHARLES
My conscience is become my enemy,
And will pursue me more than Acton can.

SUSAN
O fly, sweet brother.

SIR CHARLES   Shall I fly from thee?
What, Sue, art weary of my company?   75

SUSAN
Fly from your foe.

57 SUSAN ed. (*om.* Qq.). See Note on the Text, pp. xxx–xxxi
57 *among* Q1 (mong Q3)
58 *jest* Q1 (iests Q3)
59 *rumour of this fear* news of this feared happening
59 *stretched to* reached
71 *Unto . . . the law* to the full extent of the punishments decreed by law
72 *my* Q1 (mine Q3)
75 *What, Sue* ed. (What *Iane* Q1; Why *Sue* Q3)

SIR CHARLES   You, sister, are my friend,
  And flying you, I shall pursue my end.

SUSAN
  Your company is as my eyeball dear;
  Being far from you, no comfort can be near: 80
  Yet fly to save your life. What would I care
  To spend my future age in black despair,
  So you were safe? And yet to live one week
  Without my brother Charles, through every cheek
  My streaming tears would downwards run so rank
  Till they could set on either side a bank,   85
  And in the midst a channel; so my face
  For two salt water brooks shall still find place.

SIR CHARLES
  Thou shalt not weep so much, for I will stay
  In spite of danger's teeth. I'll live with thee,
  Or I'll not live at all. I will not sell   90
  My country, and my father's patrimony,
  No, thy sweet sight, for a vain hope of life.

                    Enter SHERIFF *with* OFFICERS

SHERIFF
  Sir Charles, I am made the unwilling instrument
  Of your attach and apprehension.
  I am sorry that the blood of innocent men   95
  Should be of you exacted. It was told me
  That you were guarded with a troop of friends,
  And therefore I come armed.

SIR CHARLES   O Master Sheriff,
  I came into the field with many friends,
  But see, they all have left me; only one   100
  Clings to my sad misfortune, my dear sister.
  I know you for an honest gentleman;
  I yield my weapons and submit to you.
  Convey me where you please.

SHERIFF   To prison then,
  To answer for the lives of these dead men.   105

---

88 *shalt* Q1 (shall Q3)
94 *attach* arrest
96 *exacted* Q1 (enacted Q3). 'Exacted' here means shed or spilled
98 *I come armed* Q1 (came thus arm'd Q3)
99 *many* Q3 (man Q1)

SUSAN
O God! O God!

SIR CHARLES   Sweet sister, every strain
Of sorrow from your heart augments my pain;
Your grief abounds and hits against my breast.

SHERIFF
Sir, will you go?

SIR CHARLES   Even where it likes you best.

[*Exeunt*]

SCENE IV

Enter MASTER FRANKFORD *in a study*

FRANKFORD
How happy am I amongst other men
That in my mean estate embrace content.
I am a gentleman, and by my birth
Companion with a king; a king's no more.
I am possessed of many fair revenues,   5
Sufficient to maintain a gentleman.
Touching my mind, I am studied in all arts;
The riches of my thoughts and of my time
Have been a good proficient. But the chief
Of all the sweet felicities on earth,   10
I have a fair, a chaste, and loving wife,
Perfection all, all truth, all ornament.
If man on earth may truly happy be,
Of these at once possessed, sure I am he.

Enter NICK

---

108 *abounds* overflows
    s.d. *in a study* i.e. deep in thought
  2 *mean* modest
  9 *have been ... proficient* have made profitable use, or have been one who has made
    good use
 12 *all ornament* composed of qualities conferring beauty, grace, or honour
 14 *at once* simultaneously, at the same time

---

  4 *companion ... no more* Frankford's allusion to his courtly youth is unique in the
    play. He seems proud equally of his connections with royalty, and of his present
    independence

NICK
    Sir, there's a gentleman attends without to speak with   15
    you.

FRANKFORD
    On horseback?

NICK
    Ay, on horseback

FRANKFORD
    Entreat him to alight; I will attend him.
    Knowest thou him, Nick?

NICK   I know him; his name's Wendoll.   20
    It seems he comes in haste. His horse is booted
    Up to the flank in mire, himself all spotted
    And stained with plashing. Sure he rid in fear
    Or for a wager; horse and man both sweat.
    I ne'er saw two in such a smoking heat.   25

FRANKFORD
    Entreat him in. About it instantly.   [*Exit* NICK]
    This Wendoll I have noted, and his carriage
    Hath pleased me much. By observation
    I have noted many good deserts in him:
    He's affable, and seen in many things,   30
    Discourses well, a good companion,
    And though of small means, yet a gentleman
    Of a good house, somewhat pressed by want.
    I have preferred him to a second place
    In my opinion, and my best regard.   35

Enter WENDOLL, ANNE, and NICK

ANNE
    O Master Frankford, Master Wendoll here
    Brings you the strangest news that ere you heard.

FRANKFORD
    What news, sweet wife? What news good Master
        Wendoll?

18 *Ay* I Q1 (Yes Q3)
19 *I will* Q1 (and ile Q3)
20 *I know him* Q1 (Know him Q3)
23 *plashing* splashing
27 *carriage* conduct
30 *seen* (well) versed
34 *preferred* promoted
36 s.d. ANNE *Mistress Frankford* Q3 (*Maister Frankford* Q1)

WENDOLL
You knew the match made 'twixt Sir Francis Acton and
Sir Charles Mountford?

FRANKFORD   True, with their hounds and hawks.   40

WENDOLL
The matches were both played.

FRANKFORD   Ha! and which won?

WENDOLL
Sir Francis, your wife's brother, had the worst,
And lost the wager.

FRANKFORD   Why, the worse his chance.
Perhaps the fortune of some other day
Will change his luck.

ANNE   O, but you hear not all.   45
Sir Francis lost, and yet was loth to yield.
In brief, the two knights grew to difference,
From words to blows, and so to banding sides,
Where valorous Sir Charles slew in his spleen
Two of your brother's men: his falconer   50
And his good huntsman, whom he loved so well.
More men were wounded, no more slain outright.

FRANKFORD
Now, trust me, I am sorry for the knight.
But is my brother safe?

WENDOLL   All whole and sound,
His body not being blemished with one wound.   55
But poor Sir Charles is to the prison led,
To answer at th'assize for them that's dead.

FRANKFORD
I thank your pains, sir. Had the news been better
Your will was to have brought it, Master Wendoll.

---

47 *In brief* Q1 (At length Q3)
58-9 *Had the news... it i.e.* You would have brought us more pleasing news had you
    any choice in the matter

---

41 *both* There is no indication that both matches were played, unless that with the
    hounds preceded the fatal match with hawks (see Scene III)
46 ANNE Q1, Q3. It was Baskervill who plausibly reassigned this speech to Wendoll on
    the strength of the reference to 'your brother' in line 51, but Anne might as well be
    retelling what Wendoll has just told her off-stage

Sir Charles will find hard friends; his case is heinous,   60
And will be most severely censured on.
I am sorry for him. Sir, a word with you.
I know you, sir, to be a gentleman
In all things, your possibilities but mean.
Please you to use my table and my purse,   65
They are yours.

WENDOLL   O Lord, sir, I shall never deserve it!

FRANKFORD
O sir, disparage not your worth too much.
You are full of quality and fair desert.
Choose of my men which shall attend on you,
And he is yours. I will allow you, sir,   70
Your man, your gelding, and your table,
All at my own charge. Be my companion.

WENDOLL
Master Frankford, I have oft been bound to you
By many favours; this exceeds them all
That I shall never merit your least favour.   75
But when your last remembrance I forget,
Heaven at my soul exact that weighty debt.

FRANKFORD
There needs no protestation, for I know you
Virtuous, and therefore grateful. Prithee Nan,
Use him with all thy loving'st courtesy.   80

ANNE
As far as modesty may well extend,
It is my duty to receive your friend.

FRANKFORD
To dinner, come sir; from this present day,
Welcome to me forever. Come away!

[*Exeunt* FRANKFORD, ANNE *and* WENDOLL]

---

60 *find hard friends* find support difficult to come by
64 *possibilities* Q1 (possibility Q3)
69 *on you* Q1 (you sir Q3)
71 *table* board, meals
76 *your last remembrance i.e.* this latest kindness

---

81 *As far… extend* Perhaps Anne's reservation here indicates her own anticipation of
the moral difficulty to come

NICK

    I do not like this fellow by no means: 85
    I never see him but my heart still earns.
    Zounds, I could fight with him, yet know not why.
    The Devil and he are all one in my eye.

               Enter JENKIN

JENKIN

    O Nick, what gentleman is that comes to lie at our house?
    My master allows him one to wait on him, and I believe it   90
    will fall to thy lot.

NICK

    I love my master, by these hilts I do,
    But rather than I'll ever come to serve him,
    I'll turn away my master.

               Enter SISLY

SISLY

    Nicklas, where are you Nicklas? You must come in,   95
    Nicklas, and help the young gentleman off with his boots.

NICK

    If I pluck off his boots, I'll eat the spurs,
    And they shall stick fast in my throat like burrs.

               Exit NICK

SISLY

    Then Jenkin, come you?

JENKIN

    'Tis no boot for me to deny it. My master hath given me a   100
    coat here, but he takes pains himself to brush it once or
    twice a day with a holly-wand.

85 *not* Q3 (nor Q1)
86 *earns* grieves (Van Fossen), but the word also means 'curdles' (*OED* v²) and the
    sense of 'turns sour' figuratively seems appropriate here
87 *Zounds* God's wounds
88 *my* Q1 (mine Q3)
88 Q3 gives an exit for Nick here
89 *that* Q1 (that that Q3)
92 *hilts i.e.* of his dagger
93 *him i.e.* Wendoll
96 *young* Q1 (*omitted* Q3)
100 *'Tis* Q1 (Nay 'tis Q3)
100 *boot* avail (also a pun)
101 *coat i.e.* the servant's livery
101–2 *to brush… holly-wand i.e.* to give me a beating

SISLY

Come, come, make haste, that you may wash your hands
again, and help to serve in dinner.

JENKIN

[*To audience*] You may see, my masters, though it be   105
afternoon with you, 'tis but early days with us, for we
have not dined yet. Stay but a little, I'll but go in and help
to bear up the first course and come to you again
presently.

Exeunt JENKIN *and* SISLY

SCENE V

Enter MALBY *and* CRANWELL

MALBY

This is the sessions day. Pray, can you tell me
How young Sir Charles hath sped? Is he acquit,
Or must he try the law's strict penalty?

CRANWELL

He's cleared of all, spite of his enemies,
Whose earnest labours was to take his life.   5
But in this suit of pardon he hath spent
All the revenues that his father left him,
And he is now turned a plain countryman,
Reformed in all things. See, sir, here he comes.

Enter SIR CHARLES *and his* KEEPER

KEEPER

Discharge your fees and you are then at freedom.   10

---

3 *try* endure, suffer
8 *a plain countryman i.e.* he is no longer a landlord
9 *Reformed* changed, transformed
9 s.d. CHARLES Q3 (Francis Q1)

106–107 *afternoon...yet* Plays were performed in the afternoon, though the action of
the play has only reached noon, the usual dinner hour. The willingness to draw
attention to the discrepancy says something about the Elizabethan conventions of
theatrical realism
109 *presently* A break in the action, an act division or perhaps a brief interval, seems to
be implied here. In that case, the word would mean 'shortly' rather than its normal
17th century scene of 'immediately'. There is a break in time between the events of
this scene and those of the next, which are quickly located in time by the opening
sentence

SIR CHARLES
  Here, Master Keeper, take the poor remainder
  Of all the wealth I have. My heavy foes
  Have made my purse light, but, alas, to me
  'Tis wealth enough that you have set me free.

MALBY
  God give you joy of your delivery;   15
  I am glad to see you abroad, Sir Charles.

SIR CHARLES
  The poorest knight in England, Master Malby;
  My life hath cost me all the patrimony
  My father left his son. Well, God forgive them
  That are the authors of my penury.   20

                    Enter SHAFTON

SHAFTON
  Sir Charles, a hand, a hand—at liberty!
  Now by the faith I owe, I am glad to see it.
  What want you? Wherein may I pleasure you?

SIR CHARLES
  O me! O most unhappy gentleman!
  I am not worthy to have friends stirred up   25
  Whose hands may help me in this plunge of want.
  I would I were in heaven to inherit there
  Th'immortal birthright which my Saviour keeps,
  And by no unthrift can be bought and sold;
  For here on earth, what pleasures should we trust?   30

SHAFTON
  To rid you from these contemplations
  Three hundred pounds you shall receive of me—
  Nay, five for fail. Come sir, the sight of gold
  Is the most sweet receipt for melancholy,
  And will revive your spirits. You shall hold law   35
  With your proud adversaries. Tush, let Frank Acton

---

16 *abroad* out of confinement, at liberty
18 *the* Q1 (my Q3)
21 s.d. SHAFTON Q1 (speech-head omitted in Q3). See Note on the Text, pp. xxx–xxxi
22 *owe* own, profess
26 *plunge of want* crises of poverty
28 *immortal birthright* the promise of eternal life
29 *unthrift* spendthrift
33 *for fail* in order to be sure
34 *receipt* recipe, antidote

Wage with knighthoodlike expense with me,
And he will sink, he will. Nay, good Sir Charles,
Applaud your fortune, and your fair escape
From all these perils.

SIR CHARLES   O sir, they have undone me!   40
Two thousand and five hundred pound a year
My father at his death possessed me of,
All which the envious Acton made me spend.
And notwithstanding all this large expense,
I had much ado to gain my liberty;   45
And I have now only a house of pleasure,
With some five hundred pounds, reserved
Both to maintain me and my loving sister.

SHAFTON
[*Aside*] That must I have; it lies convenient for me.
If I can fasten but one finger on him,   50
With my full hand I'll grip him to the heart.
'Tis not for love I proffered him this coin,
But for my gain and pleasure. [*To* SIR CHARLES] Come,
    Sir Charles,
I know you have need of money; take my offer.

SIR CHARLES
Sir, I accept it, and remain indebted,   55
Even to the best of my unable power.
Come, gentlemen, and see it tendered down.

Exeunt

SCENE VI

Enter WENDOLL, *melancholy*

WENDOLL
I am a villain if I apprehend
But such a thought; then, to attempt the deed—
Slave, thou art damned without redemption.

---

37 *Wage with knighthoodlike* Q1 (Wage his Knight-hood-like Q3)
46 *now only* Q1 (only now Q3)
46 *house of pleasure* a house used for recreation or pleasure, a summer-house
56 *unable* feeble
57 *tendered down* paid according to legal form (something more contractual than the
     OED's simple 'laid down in payment' seems implied here)
 1 WENDOLL Q1 (*omitted* Q3) See the Note on the Text p. xxx–xxxi
 1 *apprehend* think, conceive, formulate

I'll drive away this passion with a song.
A song! Ha, ha! A song, as if, fond man,   5
Thy eyes could swim in laughter when thy soul
Lies drenched and drowned in red tears of blood.
I'll pray, and see if God within my heart
Plant better thoughts. Why, prayers are meditations,
And when I meditate—O God forgive me—   10
It is on her divine perfections.
I will forget her; I will arm myself
Not to entertain a thought of love to her;
And when I come by chance into her presence,
I'll hale these balls until my eye-strings crack,   15
From being pulled and drawn to look that way.

Enter over the stage FRANKFORD, ANNE, *and* NICK

O God! O God! with what a violence
I am hurried to my own destruction.
There goest thou, the most perfect'st man
That ever England bred a gentleman;   20
And shall I wrong his bed? Thou God of thunder,
Stay, in thy thoughts of vengeance and of wrath,
Thy great, almighty and all-judging hand
From speedy execution on a villain,
A villain, and a traitor to his friend.   25

Enter JENKIN *[unobserved by* WENDOLL]

JENKIN
    Did your worship call?

WENDOLL
    [*Unhearing*] He doth maintain me; he allows me largely
    Money to spend—

JENKIN
    [*Aside*] By my faith, so do not you me; I cannot get a cross
    of you.   30

WENDOLL
    My gelding and my man.

JENKIN
    [*Aside*] That's Sorrel and I.

---

5 *fond* foolish
15 *balls* eyeballs
18 *my* Q1 (mine Q3)
19 *perfect'st* Q1 (perfect's Q3)
27 *largely* generously
29 *cross* a coin (bearing the mark of a cross)

WENDOLL
This kindness grows of no alliance 'twixt us

JENKIN
[*Aside*] Nor is my service of any great acquaintance.

WENDOLL
I never bound him to me by desert;   35
Of a mere stranger, a poor gentleman,
A man by whom in no kind he could gain,
He hath placed me in the height of all his thoughts,
Made me companion with the best and chiefest
In Yorkshire. He cannot eat without me,   40
Nor laugh without me; I am to his body
As necessary as his digestion,
And equally do make him whole or sick.
And shall I wrong this man? Base man! Ingrate!
Hast thou the power straight with thy gory hands   45
To rip thy image from his bleeding heart?
To scratch thy name from out the holy book
Of his remembrance, and to wound his name
That holds thy name so dear, or rend his heart
To whom thy heart was joined and knit together?   50
And yet I must. Then, Wendoll, be content.
Thus villains, when they would, cannot repent.

JENKIN
[*Aside*] What a strange humour is my new master in. Pray
God he be not mad. If he should be so, I should never
have any mind to serve him in Bedlam. It may be he is   55
mad for missing of me.

WENDOLL
[*Seeing* JENKIN] What, Jenkin? Where's your mistress?

JENKIN
Is your worship married?

WENDOLL
Why dost thou ask?

---

35 *me* Q3 (be Q1)
36 *mere* entire, complete
38 *He hath... thoughts* Q1 (And he hath plac'd me in his highest thoughts Q3)
50 *joined and knit* Q1 (knit and ioyn'd Q3)
55 *Bedlam* the famous London asylum for the insane

---

34 *of any great acquaintance i.e.* because I have known Wendoll for a particularly long
   time. (Wendoll's word 'kindness' is matched by Jenkin's 'service', and 'alliance' by
   'acquaintance', in parodic deflation.)

JENKIN

    Because you are my master, and if I have a mistress, I   60
    would be glad, like a good servant, to do my duty to her.

WENDOLL

    I mean where's Mistress Frankford?

JENKIN

    Marry, sir, her husband is riding out of town, and she
    went very lovingly to bring him on his way to horse. Do
    you see, sir, here she comes, [*Aside*] and here I go.   65

WENDOLL

    Vanish.   *Exit* JENKIN

Enter ANNE

ANNE

    You are well met, sir. Now in troth my husband
    Before he took horse had a great desire
    To speak with you. We sought about the house,
    Hallowed into the fields, sent every way,   70
    But could not meet you. Therefore he enjoined me
    To do unto you his most kind commends.
    Nay, more; he wills you as you prize his love,
    Or hold in estimation his kind friendship,
    To make bold in his absence and command   75
    Even as himself were present in the house,
    For you must keep his table, use his servants,
    And be a present Frankford in his absence.

WENDOLL

    I thank him for his love.
    [*Aside*] Give me a name, you whose infectious tongues   80
    Are tipped with gall and poison; as you would
    Think on a man that had your father slain,
    Murdered thy children, made your wives base strumpets,
    So call me. Call me so? Print in my face
    The most stigmatic title of a villain,   85
    For hatching treason to so true a friend.

---

62 *where's Mistress* Q1 (Mistris Q3)

70 *Hallowed* Q1 (Hollow'd Q3)

72 *kind* Q3 (kinds Q1)
    commends compliments

77 *keep* preside over, take care of, take charge of, maintain

83 *thy* Q1 (your Q3)

84 *Call… Print* i.e. Not only do I deserve to be called by such a name, but to have it
    printed in my face

85 *stigmatic* infamous, severely condemnatory

ANNE

Sir, you are much beholding to my husband.
You are a man most dear in his regard.

WENDOLL

I am bound unto your husband and you too.
[*Aside*] I will not speak to wrong a gentleman   90
Of that good estimation, my kind friend.
I will not! Zounds, I will not! I may choose,
And I will choose! Shall I be so misled?
Or shall I purchase to my father's crest
The motto of a villain? If I say   95
I will not do it, what thing can enforce me?
Who can compel me? What sad destiny
Hath such command upon my yielding thoughts?
I will not! Ha! some fury pricks me on;
The swift fates drag me at their chariot wheel,   100
And hurry me to mischief. Speak I must—
Injure myself, wrong her, deceive his trust.

ANNE

Are you not well, sir, that you seem thus troubled?
There is sedition in your countenance!

WENDOLL

And in my heart, fair angel, chaste and wise.   105
I love you—start not, speak not, answer not.
I love you—nay, let me speak the rest.
Bid me to swear, and I will call to record
The host of heaven.

ANNE   The host of heaven forbid
Wendoll should hatch such a disloyal thought.   110

WENDOLL

Such is my fate; to this suit I was born:
To wear rich pleasure's crown, or fortune's scorn.

92 *Zounds* God's wounds
97 *Who* Q1 (What Q3)
97 *sad* causing sorrow, distressing
103 *you seem* Q1 (ye seeme Q3)
104 *sedition* internal strife or tumult
107 *me* Q3 (we Q1)

94–5 *crest . . . villain* The crest and motto were the heraldic marks of gentility; the word
'villain' revives in a pun its etymological relation to 'villein' = feudal serf

ANNE
My husband loves you.

WENDOLL   I know it.

ANNE   He esteems you
Even as his brain, his eye-ball, or his heart.

WENDOLL
I have tried it.   115

ANNE
His purse is your exchequer, and his table
Doth freely serve you.

WENDOLL   So I have found it.

ANNE
O with what face of brass, what brow of steel,
Can you unblushing speak this to the face
Of the espoused wife of so dear a friend?   120
It is my husband that maintains your state;
Will you dishonour him? I am his wife
That in your power hath left his whole affairs;
It is to me you speak?

WENDOLL   O speak no more,
For more than this I know and have recorded   125
Within the red-leaved table of my heart.
Fair, and of all beloved, I was not fearful
Bluntly to give my life into your hand,
And at one hazard all my earthly means.
Go, tell your husband; he will turn me off,   130
And I am then undone. I care not, I—
'Twas for your sake. Perchance in rage he'll kill me.
I care not—'twas for you. Say I incur
The general name of villain through the world,
Of traitor to my friend—I care not, I.   135
Beggary, shame, death, scandal, and reproach,
For you I'll hazard all—what care I?
For you I'll live, and in your love I'll die.

115 *tried* put to the proof
116 *your* Q3 (you Q1)
126 *table* notebook
129 *at one hazard* at once put at risk
137 *what care* Q1 (why what care Q3)
138 *live* Q1 (loue Q3)

ANNE

    You move me, sir, to passion and to pity.
    The love I bear my husband is as precious   140
    As my soul's health.

WENDOLL   I love your husband too,
    And for his love I will engage my life.
    Mistake me not, the augmentation
    Of my sincere affection borne to you
    Doth no whit lessen my regard of him.   145
    I will be secret, lady, close as night,
    And not the light of one small glorious star
    Shall shine here in my forehead to bewray
    That act of night.

ANNE   What shall I say?
    My soul is wandering, and hath lost her way.   150
    O Master Wendoll, O.

WENDOLL   Sigh not, sweet saint,
    For every sigh you breathe draws from my heart
    A drop of blood.

ANNE   I ne'er offended yet.
    My fault, I fear, will in my brow be writ.
    Women that fall not quite bereft of grace   155
    Have their offences noted in their face.
    I blush and am ashamed. O Master Wendoll,
    Pray God I be not born to curse your tongue
    That hath enchanted me. This maze I am in
    I fear will prove the labyrinth of sin.   160

Enter NICK [*unnoticed by* ANNE *and* WENDOLL]

WENDOLL

    The path of pleasure, and the gate to bliss,
    Which on your lips I knock at with a kiss.

[*Kisses* ANNE]

NICK

    [*Aside*] I'll kill the rogue.

146 *close* secretive
148 *bewray* betray, expose, reveal
149 *act of night* i.e. adultery
154 *my* Q3 (*omitted* Q)
159 *maze* a pun (a) state of bewilderment (b) labyrinth (in line 160)

152-3 *every sigh... blood* An exploitation of the popular belief that a sigh cost one's
    heart a drop of blood. (Van Fossen cites Donne's use in the song 'Sweetest love I do
    not go': 'When thou sigh'st, thou sigh'st not winde,/But sigh'st my soule away.')

WENDOLL
  Your husband is from home, your bed's no blab—
  Nay, look not down and blush.

Exeunt ANNE *and* WENDOLL

NICK   Zounds, I'll stab.   165
  Ay, Nick, was it thy chance to come just in the nick.
  I love my master, and I hate that slave;
  I love my mistress, but these tricks I like not.
  My master shall not pocket up this wrong;
  I'll eat my fingers first. What sayest thou metal?   170
            [Drawing his dagger]
  Does not the rascal Wendoll go on legs
  That thou must cut off? Hath he not hamstrings
  That thou must hough? Nay metal, thou shalt stand
  To all I say. I'll henceforth turn a spy,
  And watch them in their close conveyances.   175
  I never looked for better of that rascal
  Since he came miching first into our house.
  It is that Satan hath corrupted her,
  For she was fair and chaste. I'll have an eye
  In all their gestures. Thus I think of them: 180
  If they proceed as they have done before,
  Wendoll's a knave, my mistress is a etcetera.

Exit

164 *blab* tell-tale
165 *Zounds* God's wounds
166 *in the nick* at the critical moment (punning on his name)
169 *pocket up* submit to, endure meekly or in ignorance
171 *the* Q1 (that Q3)
173 *hough* cut (the tendons behind the knee), disable
173 *shalt* Q1 (shall Q3)
175 *close conveyances* secret communications
177 *miching* skulking, pretending poverty
180 *gestures* actions, deeds
182 *etcetera* Q1 (— — Q3)

SCENE VII

Enter SIR CHARLES *and* SUSAN

SIR CHARLES
    Sister, you see we are driven to hard shift
    To keep this poor house we have left unsold.
    I am now enforced to follow husbandry,
    And you to milk. And do we not live well?
    Well, I thank God.

SUSAN   O brother, here's a change   5
    Since old Sir Charles died in our father's house.

SIR CHARLES
    All things on earth thus change, some up, some down;
    Content's a kingdom, and I wear that crown.

Enter SHAFTON *with a* SERGEANT

SHAFTON
    Good morrow, good morrow, Sir Charles. What, with
        your sister,
    Plying your husbandry? Sergeant, stand off.   10
    You have a pretty house here, and a garden
    And goodly ground about it. Since it lies
    So near a lordship that I lately bought,
    I would fain buy it of you. I will give you—

SIR CHARLES
    O pardon me, this house successively   15
    Hath 'longed to me and my progenitors
    Three hundred year. My great-great-grandfather,
    He in whom first our gentle style began,
    Dwelt here, and in this ground increased this mole-hill
    Unto that mountain which my father left me.   20

---

1 *hard shift* difficult expedients
3 *husbandry i.e.* farming
9 SHAFTON Q1 (*omitted* Q3). See Note on the Text p. xxx–xxxi
9 *morrow, good morrow* Q1 (morrow, morrow Q3)
10 *Sergeant* a legal officer charged with the arrest of offenders and summoning persons
   before court
13 *lordship* estate, domain (land belonging to a lord)
16 *'longed* belonged
17 *year* Q1 (yeeres Q3)
18 *gentle style* status of gentility

Where he the first of all our house began,
I now the last will end and keep this house,
This virgin title never yet deflowered
By any unthrift of the Mountford's line.
In brief, I will not sell it for more gold   25
Than you could hide or pave the ground withal.

SHAFTON
Ha, ha! a proud mind and a beggar's purse.
Where's my three hundred pounds, beside the use?
I have brought it to an execution
By course of law. What? Is my money ready?   30

SIR CHARLES
An execution, sir, and never tell me
You put my bond in suit? You deal extremely.

SHAFTON
Sell me the land and I'll acquit you straight.

SIR CHARLES
Alas, alas! 'Tis all trouble hath left me
To cherish me and my poor sister's life.   35
If this were sold our means should then be quite
Razed from the bead-roll of gentility.
You see what hard shift we have made to keep it
Allied still to our own name. This palm you see
Labour hath glowed within; her silver brow,   40
That never tasted a rough winter's blast

---

23 *title* legal right to possession
28 *beside* Q1 (besides Q3)
28 *use* interest
29 *an* Q1 (*omitted* Q3)
29 *execution* legal seizure of goods or person of a defaulting debtor
30 *money* Q1 (monies Q3)
32 *put... in suit* set the law in motion concerning my bond
32 *extremely* with a very great degree of severity
35 *cherish* support, foster
36 *means* Q1, Q3 (names *Dodsley's emendation*)
37 *Razed* erased
37 *bead-roll* list

---

40 *glowed* Sturgess proposed that Heywood wrote 'gald', that it was misread by the
1607 compositor as 'gloud' (=gloved), and subsequently changed to 'glow'd' by
the compositor of 1617. See K. M. Sturgess, 'The Early Quartos of Heywood's *A
woman killed with kindness*', in *The Library* (fifth series), vol. XXV, 2 (1970), pp.
93–104, and Note on the Text pp. xxxii–xxxiii

Without a mask or fan, doth with a grace
Defy cold winter and his storms outface.

SUSAN

Sir, we feed sparing and we labour hard,
We lie uneasy, to reserve to us   45
And our succession this small plot of ground.

SIR CHARLES

I have so bent my thoughts to husbandry
That I protest I scarcely can remember
What a new fashion is, how silk or satin
Feels in my hand. Why, pride is grown to us   50
A mere, mere stranger. I have quite forgot
The names of all that ever waited on me;
I cannot name ye any of my hounds,
Once from whose echoing mouths I heard all the music
That e'er my heart desired. What should I say?   55
To keep this place I have changed myself away.

SHAFTON

Arrest him at my suit. Actions and actions
Shall keep thee in perpetual bondage fast.
Nay, more, I'll sue thee by a late appeal,
And call thy former life in question.   60
The keeper is my friend; thou shalt have irons
And usage such as I'll deny to dogs. Away with him!

SIR CHARLES

You are too timorous, but trouble is my master
And I will serve him truly. My kind sister,   65
Thy tears are of no force to mollify
This flinty man. Go to my father's brother,
My kinsmen and allies, entreat them from me
To ransom me from this injurious man
That seeks my ruin.

---

42 *mask or fan i.e.* as protections against the weather, the effects of which on the
   complexion were not then valued by the upper or wealthier classes
45 *uneasy* uncomfortably
45 *reserve* preserve
51 *mere* absolute, complete
54 *the* Q1 (*omitted* Q3)
57 *actions i.e.* legal actions
58 *perpetual* Q1 (continuall Q3)
59 *late appeal i.e.* revived charge (of killing Sir Francis's men)
64 *You* Q1 (Ye Q3)
64 *timorous* fearful of my resistance, or possibly the sense 'dreadful, terrible' favoured
   by Van Fossen

SHAFTON   Come, irons, irons, away!   70
  I'll see thee lodged far from the sight of day.

    Exeunt [SHAFTON *and* SERGEANT *with* SIR CHARLES *in irons*]
Enter SIR FRANCIS *and* MALBY [*unseen by* SUSAN *and not noticing
her*]

SUSAN
  My heart's so hardened with the frost of grief
  Death cannot pierce it through. Tyrant too fell!
  So lead the fiends condemned souls to hell.

SIR FRANCIS
  Again to prison! Malby, hast thou seen   75
  A poor slave better tortured? Shall we hear
  The music of his voice cry from the grate
  'Meat for the Lord's sake'? No, no, yet I am not
  Throughly revenged. They say he hath a pretty wench
  Unto his sister: shall I, in mercy sake   80
  To him and to his kindred, bribe the fool
  To shame herself by lewd dishonest lust.
  I'll proffer largely, but the deed being done
  I'll smile to see her base confusion.

MALBY
  Methinks, Sir Francis, you are full revenged   85
  For greater wrongs than he can proffer you.
  See where the poor sad gentlewoman stands.

SIR FRANCIS
  Ha, ha! Now I will flout her poverty,
  Deride her fortunes, scoff her base estate.
  My very soul the name of Mountford hates.   90
  But stay, my heart, O what a look did fly
  To strike my soul through with thy piercing eye.
  I am enchanted, all my spirits are fled,
  And with one glance my envious spleen struck dead.

70 *irons, irons, away* Q1 (irons, irons; come away Q3)
71 s.d. *Enter...* This entrance appears after Susan's speech (11.72–74) in Q3
73 *fell* cruel, ruthless
77 *grate* prison bars
78 *Lord's sake* Q3 (Lord sake Q1)
80 *Unto* Q1 (To Q3)
80 *mercy* Q1 (my mercy Q3)
82 *dishonest* dishonourable, unchaste
83 *largely* generously
88 *I will* Q1 (will I Q3)
90 *hates* Q1 (hate Q3)
91 *O what* ed. (or what Q1, Q3)

SUSAN
    [*Seeing them*] Acton, that seeks our blood!

                                 Runs away

SIR FRANCIS   O chaste and fair!   95

MALBY
    Sir Francis, why Sir Francis? Zounds, in a trance?
    Sir Francis, what cheer man? Come, come, how is't?

SIR FRANCIS
    Was she not fair? Or else this judging eye
    Cannot distinguish beauty.

MALBY   She was fair.

SIR FRANCIS
    She was an angel in a mortal's shape,   100
    And ne'er descended from old Mountford's line.
    But soft, soft, let me call my wits together.
    A poor, poor wench, to my great adversary
    Sister, whose very souls denounce stern war
    One against other? How now, Frank, turned fool   105
    Or madman, whether? By no! master of
    My perfect senses and directest wits.
    Then why should I be in this violent humour
    Of passion and of love, and with a person
    So different every way, and so opposed   110
    In all contractions and still warring actions?
    Fie, fie, how I dispute against my soul.
    Come, come, I'll gain her, or in her fair quest
    Purchase my soul free and immortal rest.

                                Exeunt

---

95 s.d. *Runs* Q3 (Run Q1)
 96 *Zounds* God's wounds (*omitted* Q3)
104 *denounce* declare, announce
105 *One* Q1 (Each Q3)
107 *directest* most straightforward, unambiguous
111 *contractions* counteractions (not in *OED* in this sense)

SCENE VIII

Enter THREE *or* FOUR SERVINGMEN [*including* NICK *and* SPIGGOT *the Butler*], *one with a voider and a wooden knife to take away all, another the salt and bread, another the table-cloth and napkins, another the carpet.* JENKIN *with two lights after them*

JENKIN
So, march in order and retire in battle 'ray. My master
and the guests have supped already, all's taken away.
Here now spread for the servingmen in the hall. Butler, it
belongs to your office.

SPIGGOT
I know it, Jenkin. What do you call the gentleman that   5
supped there tonight?

JENKIN
Who, my master?

SPIGGOT
No, no, Master Wendoll, he is a daily guest. I mean the
gentleman that came but this afternoon.

JENKIN
His name is Master Cranwell. God's light, hark within   10
there! My master calls to lay more billets on the fire.
Come, come! Lord, how we that are in office here in
the house are troubled. One spread the carpet in the
parlour and stand ready to snuff the lights; the rest be
ready to prepare their stomachs. More lights in the hall   15
there! Come Nicklas.

                               [*Exeunt all but* NICK]

    s.d. *away all* Q1 (away Q3)
  1 *'ray* Q1 (array Q3)
  5 *do you* Q1 (de'ye Q3)
  8 s.d. SPIGGOT ed. (*But.* Q1; *Wen* Q3)
 11 *billets* thick pieces of wood
 11 *on* Q1 (vppon Q3)
 13 *spread the carpet i.e.* on the table, rather than the floor
_____

    s.d. THREE *or* FOUR Q1, Q3. This reading suggests the authorial foul papers that lie
    behind the first edition. No theatrical document would allow itself this measure of
    imprecision

NICK

    I cannot eat, but had I Wendoll's heart
    I would eat that; the rogue grows impudent.
    O I have seen such vile notorious tricks,
    Ready to make my eyes dart from my head.   20
    I'll tell my master, by this air I will;
    Fall what may fall, I'll tell him. Here he comes.

Enter FRANKFORD *as it were brushing the crumbs from his clothes*
with a napkin, and newly risen from supper

FRANKFORD

    Nicklas, what make you here? Why are not you
    At supper in the hall there with your fellows.

NICK

    Master, I stayed your rising from the board   25
    To speak with you.

FRANKFORD   Be brief then, gentle Nicklas,
    My wife and guests attend me in the parlour.
    Why dost thou pause? Now Nicklas, you want money,
    And unthrift-like would eat into your wages
    Ere you have earned it. Here's, sir, half-a-crown,   30
    Play the good husband and away to supper.

NICK

    [*Aside*] By this hand, an honourable gentleman! I will not
    see him wronged. Sir, I have served you long. You
    entertained me seven years before your beard. You knew
    me, sir, before you knew my mistress.   35

FRANKFORD

    What of this, good Nicklas?

NICK

    I never was a make-bate or a knave.
    I have no fault but one—I am given to quarrel,

22 s.d. *and* Q1 (as Q3)
24 *there with* Q1 (among Q3)
25 *stayed* waited until
27 *attend* await
28 *want* lack
29 *unthrift-like* spendthriftlike
30 *Here's, sir* Q1 (heere sirs Q3)
31 *Play the good husband i.e.* manage the money well, be thrifty (but ironically exploiting the play on the word 'husband')
34 *entertained* retained in service, employed
37 *make-bate* mischief-maker, breeder of quarrels

But not with women. I will tell you, master,
That which will make your heart leap from your breast,   40
Your hair to startle from your head, your ears to tingle.

FRANKFORD
What preparation's this to dismal news?

NICK
'Sblood sir, I love you better than your wife.
I'll make it good.

FRANKFORD
Thou art a knave, and I have much ado   45
With wonted patience to contain my rage
And not to break thy pate! Thou art a knave;
I'll turn you with your base comparisons
Out of my doors.

NICK
Do, do.   50
There's not room for Wendoll and me too
Both in one house. O master, master,
That Wendoll is a villain.

FRANKFORD
Ay, saucy!   [FRANKFORD *strikes him*]

NICK
Strike, strike, do strike, yet hear me. I am no fool,   55
I know a villain when I see him act
Deeds of a villain. Master, master, that base slave
Enjoys my mistress and dishonours you.

FRANKFORD
Thou hast killed me with a weapon whose sharpened
     point
Hath pricked quite through and through my shivering
     heart.   60
Drops of cold sweat sit dangling on my hairs
Like morning's dew upon the golden flowers,
And I am plunged into a strange agony.
What didst thou say? If any word that touched
His credit or her reputation,   65

43 *'Sblood i.e.* God's blood
44 *I'll make...good i.e.* I'll justify my words. Perhaps, as Van Fossen suggests,
     Frankford threatens to strike him for him impudence
45 *Thou art* Q1 (Y'are Q3)
58 *enjoys i.e.* sexually
59 *sharpened* Q1 (sharp Q3)
63 *a strange agony* Q1 (strange agonies Q3)
65 *credit* good name, honour

It is as hard to enter my belief
As Dives into heaven.

NICK
I can gain nothing. They are two
That never wronged me. I knew before
'Twas but a thankless office, and perhaps   70
As much as my service or my life is worth.
All this I know, but this and more,
More by a thousand dangers could not hire me
To smother such a heinous wrong from you.
I saw, and I have said.   75

FRANKFORD
[*Aside*] 'Tis probable. Though blunt, yet he is honest.
Though I durst pawn my life, and on their faith
Hazard the dear salvation of my soul,
Yet in my trust I may be too secure.
May this be true? O may it, can it be?   80
Is it by any wonder possible?
Man, woman, what thing mortal may we trust,
When friends and bosom wives prove so unjust?
[*To* NICK] What instance hast thou of this strange report?

NICK
Eyes, eyes.   85

FRANKFORD
Thy eyes may be deceived I tell thee,
For should an angel from the heavens drop down
And preach this to me that thyself hast told,
He should have much ado to win belief,
In both their loves I am so confident.   90

NICK
Shall I discourse the same by circumstance?

FRANKFORD
No more; to supper, and command your fellows
To attend us and the strangers. Not a word,
I charge thee on thy life; be secret then,
For I know nothing.   95

67 *Dives* popular name for a rich man. The reference is to the parable in *Luke* xvi
71 *as my* Q1 (as is my Q3)
82 *may* Q1 (can Q3)
83 *unjust* faithless, dishonest
84 *instance* evidence
85 *Eyes, eyes* Q1 (Eyes master, eyes Q3)
93 *strangers* guests, visitors

NICK
    I am dumb. And now that I have eased my stomach,
    I will go fill my stomach.   *Exit* NICK

FRANKFORD
    Away, be gone.
    She is well born, descended nobly,
    Virtuous her education, her repute   100
    Is in the general voice of all the country
    Honest and fair, her carriage, her demeanour
    In all her actions that concern the love
    To me, her husband, modest, chaste, and godly.
    Is all this seeming gold plain copper?   105
    But he, that Judas that hath borne my purse,
    And sold me for a sin—O God, O God,
    Shall I put up these wrongs? No, shall I trust
    The bare report of this suspicious groom
    Before the double gilt, the well hatch ore   110
    Of their two hearts? No, I will loose these thoughts.
    Distraction I will banish from my brow,
    And from my looks exile sad discontent.
    Their wonted favours in my tongue shall flow.
    Till I know all, I'll nothing seem to know.   115
    Lights and a table there! Wife, Master Wendoll and
    gentle Master Cranwell—

Enter ANNE, WENDOLL, CRANWELL, NICK *and* JENKIN *with cards,
    carpet, stools and other necessaries*

---

 96 *eased my stomach* 'got it off my mind', rid myself of what stifled my appetite
108 *put up* submit to, endure, suffer quietly
109 *groom* serving-man
117 s.d. *carpet* Q1 (Carpets Q3)

---

106 *Judas that hath borne my purse* Christ's betrayer was by John's account reputed to
    have held the money-bag (*John* xiii, 29). This is the first of two allusions Frankford
    makes to Wendoll as Judas (and by implication to himself as betrayed Christ). The
    other occurs at XIII, 76–8
110 *the double gilt, the well hatch ore* The richness of 'double gilt' is intended to contrast
    with the poverty of Nick's 'bare report' (previous line), but also there is the
    inevitable pun on 'double gilt'. 'To hatch' is to inlay with gold or silver. Verity
    proposed the emendation of the quarto readings to 'well-hatched', which makes
    good sense. The phrase persists in the suggestion that gilded and decorated
    superficiality is at the same time being consciously preferred and subconsciously
    exposed by Frankford through Heywood's puns (hatched o'er = covered over?)
117 s.d. *other necessaries* a further instance of authorial papers, hardly tolerable in the
    playhouse

FRANKFORD

O you are a stranger, Master Cranwell, you,
And often baulk my house; faith, you are a churl.
Now we have supped, a table, and to cards.   120

JENKIN

A pair of cards, Nicklas, and a carpet to cover the table.
Where's Sisly with her counters and her box? Candles
and candlesticks there! Fie, we have such a household of
serving creatures! Unless it be Nick and I, there's not one
amongst them all can say boo to a goose. Well said, Nick.   125

They spread a carpet, set down lights and cards

ANNE

Come, Master Frankford, who shall take my part?

FRANKFORD

Marry, that will I, sweet wife.

WENDOLL

No, by my faith, sir, when you are together I sit out; it
must be Mistress Frankford and I, or else it is no match.

FRANKFORD

I do not like that match.   130

NICK

[*Aside*] You have no reason, marry, knowing all.

FRANKFORD

'Tis no great matter neither. Come, Master Cranwell,
shall you and I take them up?

CRANWELL

At your pleasure, sir.

FRANKFORD

I must look to you, Master Wendoll, for you will be   135
playing false—nay, so will my wife too.

---

118 *O you are a stranger, Master Cranwell, you,* Q1 (O master Cranwel, you are are [sic]
    a stranger heere Q3)
119 *baulk* avoid or pass by
121 *pair* pack
122 *counters and her box i.e.* to score the game
125 *can say boo to a goose* are capable of the simplest task (proverbial)
128 *faith, sir* Q1 (Faith Q3)
136 *playing false* (a) at cards (b) deceiving me with my wife

---

121 *carpet...table* This was the usual practice of the age. See above, line 117 s.d.
125 *Well said, Nick* well done. There is a temptation to propose this as a speech by Nick,
    perhaps garbled in the printer's copy for Q1
129 *match* This word here and in the following line takes us back to the 'matches' of the
    opening scenes. In both there is a double meaning

NICK
[*Aside*] Ay, I will be sworn she will.

ANNE
Let them that are taken playing false forfeit the set.

FRANKFORD
Content. It shall go hard but I'll take you.

CRANWELL
Gentlemen, what shall our game be?   140

WENDOLL
Master Frankford, you play best at Noddy.

FRANKFORD
You shall not find it so; indeed you shall not.

ANNE
I can play at nothing so well as Double Ruff.

FRANKFORD
If Master Wendoll and my wife be together, there's no
playing against them at double hand.   145

NICK
I can tell you, sir, the game that Master Wendoll is best
at.

WENDOLL
What game is that, Nick?

NICK
Marry, sir, Knave Out of Doors.

WENDOLL
She and I will take you at Lodam.   150

ANNE
Husband, shall we play at Saint?

137 *Ay, I* Q1 (I Q3)
139 *take you* detect you, find you out
141 *Noddy* (a) a card game (b) fool, the cuckold
143 *Double Ruff* (a) another card game, like whist (b) with 'double' in the sense of
   'deceitful, with duplicity', and 'excitement, passion' as the sense of 'ruff'
145 *double hand i.e.* (a) when they are partners in a card game (b) at duplicity
149 *Knave Out of Doors* another card game, and another play on words, in this instance
   'knave' meaning 'rascal'
150 *Lodam* a game of cards, in one form called 'losing loadum', in which the loser won
   the game (*OED*). The paradoxical nature of the game is presumably part of the
   double entendre. Van Fossen also draws attention to Florio's etymology (*OED*) in
   which he derives the name from the Italian *carica l'asino* 'load the ass', likewise
   appropriate to the play on meanings in this passage
151 *Saint* the name of this game derives from 'cent', one hundred points being required
   for a win. The anglicised title of course contributes to the series of *double entendres*,
   as the following lines indicate

FRANKFORD

[*Aside*] My saint's turned devil. [*To them*] No, we'll none
of Saint. You're best at New Cut, wife; you'll play at that.

WENDOLL

If you play at New Cut, I'm soonest hitter of any here, for
a wager.   155

FRANKFORD

[*Aside*] 'Tis me they play on; well, you may draw out.
For all your cunning, 'twill be to your shame.
I'll teach you at your New Cut, a new game.
[*To them*] Come, come.

CRANWELL

If you cannot agree upon the game, to Post and Pair.   160

WENDOLL

We shall be soonest pairs, and my good host,
When he comes late home, he must kiss the post.

FRANKFORD

Whoever wins, it shall be to thy cost.

CRANWELL

Faith, let it be Vide-ruff, and let's make honours.

FRANKFORD

If you make honours, one thing let me crave,   165
Honour the King and Queen; except the knave.

WENDOLL

Well, as you please for that. Lift who shall deal.

---

153 *New Cut* another 'old card game' (*OED*), this time with a bawdy allusion
154 *hitter* scorer, but again with a bawdy allusion in view of the sense of 'cut'
156 *draw out i.e.* both their cards and their play on him
160 *Post and Pair* a game with three cards each (hence the analogy with their triangular
relationship)
162 *post i.e.* the doorpost or gatepost; *to kiss the post* means 'to be disappointed, shut out,
excluded'
164 *Vide-ruff* the game of ruff again (see line 143), but in some variant that involves
vying or backing the trump. There is also the double sense of competing for the
lady, here (as above) representing Anne, who presumably wears one
164 *honours* in cards the four highest trumps, (ace, king, queen and knave)
166 *except* exclude
167 *Lift* cut
167 *deal* a sexual *double entendre*, picked up in the following line by Anne, meaning
'have intercourse'

---

166 *King and Queen... knave* In the *double entendre* that persists through this episode,
these cards signify Frankford, Anne and Wendoll

ANNE
  The least in sight. What are you, Master Wendoll?

WENDOLL
  [*Cutting the cards*] I am a knave.

NICK
  [*Aside*] I'll swear it.   170

ANNE
  I a queen.

FRANKFORD
  [*Aside*] A quean thou should'st say. [*To them*] Well, the
    cards are mine.
  They are the grossest pair that e'er I felt.

ANNE
  Shuffle, I'll cut. [*Aside*] Would I had never dealt.

                              [FRANKFORD *deals the cards*]

FRANKFORD
  I have lost my dealing.   175

WENDOLL
  Sir, the fault's in me.
  This queen I have more than my own, you see.
  Give me the stock.

                              [WENDOLL *deals*]

FRANKFORD   My mind's not on my game.
  [*Aside*] Many a deal I have lost, the more's your shame.
  [*To him*] You have served me a bad trick, Master
    Wendoll.   180

WENDOLL
  Sir, you must take your lot. To end this strife,
  I know I have dealt better with your wife.

FRANKFORD
  Thou hast dealt falsely then.

---

168 *least in sight i.e.* the player drawing the lowest card will be dealer, but Wendoll is in
    social terms 'the least' and likewise a sexual 'dealer'
171 *a queen* Q1 (am Queene Q3)
172 *quean* harlot
173 *felt* (a) handled (b) tested (morally)
174 *grossest pair* crudest pack (of cards), but also an allusion to the moral turpitude of
    Anne and Wendoll
174 *dealt i.e.* sexually
177 *my own* Q1 (mine owne Q3)
180 *trick* (a) hand of cards (b) deceit

ANNE
  What's trumps?

WENDOLL
  Hearts. Partner, I rub.   185

FRANKFORD
  [*Aside*] Thou robb'st me of my soul, of her chaste love;
  In thy false dealing, thou hast robbed my heart.
  Booty you play; I like a loser stand,
  Having no heart, or here, or in my hand.
  [*To them*] I will give o'er the set; I am not well.   190
  Come, who will hold my cards?

ANNE
  Not well, sweet Master Frankford?
  Alas, what ail you? 'Tis some sudden qualm.

WENDOLL
  How long have you been so, Master Frankford?

FRANKFORD
  Sir, I was lusty, and I had my health,   195
  But I grew ill when you began to deal.
  Take hence this table.

              Enter SERVANTS *to remove table, cards, etc.*

                        Gentle Master Cranwell,
  You are welcome; see your chamber at your pleasure.
  I am sorry that this megrim takes me so,
  I cannot sit and bear you company.   200
  Jenkin, some lights, and show him to his chamber.

ANNE
  A nightgown for my husband, quickly there.

              Enter SERVANT *with nightgown, and exit*

  It is some rheum or cold.

---

185 *rub* to take all the cards of one suit (*OED* v²). Also possibly 'annoy, irritate'
188 *booty i.e.* falsely in league against me. To play booty meant to play badly with
     the intention of losing the game, hence falsely betraying and victimizing one
     player
193 *qualm* feeling of illness or sickness, but also with the (unintended, but more
     accurate) sense of 'sickening fear, sinking or faintness of heart'
195 *lusty* full of healthy vigour
196 *deal* again, with a double sense, see above 11.167, 175
199 *megrim* migraine
203 *rheum* cold in the head, catarrh

WENDOLL
   Now, in good faith, this illness you have got
   By sitting late without your gown.   205

FRANKFORD
   I know it, Master Wendoll.
   Go, go to bed, lest you complain like me.
   Wife, prethee wife, into my bed-chamber.
   The night is raw and cold and rheumatic.
   Leave me my gown and light; I'll walk away my fit.   210

WENDOLL
   Sweet sir, good night.

FRANKFORD   [*Exit* WENDOLL]
   Myself, good night.

ANNE
   Shall I attend you, husband?

FRANKFORD
   No gentle wife, thou'lt catch cold in thy head.
   Prethee begone, sweet; I'll make haste to bed.   215

ANNE
   No sleep will fasten on mine eyes, you know,
   Until you come.   *Exit* ANNE

FRANKFORD   Sweet Nan, I prethee go.
   [*To* NICK] I have bethought me. Get me by degrees
   The keys of all my doors, which I will mould
   In wax, and take their fair impression,   220
   To have by them new keys. This being compassed,
   At a set hour a letter shall be brought me,
   And when they think they may securely play,
   They are nearest to danger. Nick, I must rely
   Upon thy trust and faithful secrecy.   225

NICK
   Build on my faith.

FRANKFORD   To bed then, not to rest.
   Care lodges in my brain, grief in my breast.

                                                      Exeunt

---

209 *rheumatic* likely to cause catarrh, etc.
212 *Myself i.e.* my intimate friend
214 *thou'lt catch cold* ed. (thout catcht cold Q1; thou't catch hold Q3) Van Fossen does
    not record the *hold* variant in Q3
224 *are nearest* Q1 (neerest are Q3)

SCENE IX

Enter SUSAN, OLD MOUNTFORD, SANDY, RODER *and* TYDY

OLD MOUNTFORD

    You say my nephew is in great distress—
    Who brought it to him but his own lewd life?
    I cannot spare a cross. I must confess
    He was my brother's son—why, niece, what then?
    This is no world in which to pity men.   5

SUSAN

    I was not born a beggar; though his extremes
    Enforce this language from me, I protest
    No fortune of mine own could lead my tongue
    To this base key. I do beseech you, uncle,
    For the name's sake, for Christianity,   10
    Nay, for God's sake, to pity his distress.
    He is denied the freedom of the prison,
    And in the hole is laid with men condemned.
    Plenty he hath of nothing but of irons,
    And it remains in you to free him thence.   15

OLD MOUNTFORD

    Money I cannot spare. Men should take heed.
    He lost my kindred when he fell to need.

                      Exit OLD MOUNTFORD

SUSAN

    Gold is but earth; thou earth enough shalt have
    When thou hast once took measure of thy grave.
    You know me, Master Sandy, and my suit.   20

SANDY

    I knew you, Lady, when the old man lived;
    I knew you ere your brother sold his land.
    Then you were Mistress Sue, tricked up in jewels;

  2 *lewd* wicked
  3 *cross* type of small coin
  4 *my* Q3 (me Q1)
  8 *mine own* Q3 (mine Q1)
10 *the name's sake i.e.* the family name or honour
13 *hole* dungeon, specifically one of the worst apartments of London's Counter Prison, though the action of this play seems to be laid in Yorkshire

Then you sung well, played sweetly on the flute;
But now I neither know you nor your suit.   25

                                        [*Exit* SANDY]

SUSAN

You, Master Roder, was my brother's tenant.
Rent-free he placed you in that wealthy farm
Of which you are possessed.

RODER   True, he did,
And have I not there dwelt still for his sake?
I have some business now, but without doubt   30
They that have hurled him in will help him out.

                                        Exit RODER

SUSAN

Cold comfort still. What say you, cousin Tydy?

TYDY

I say this comes of roisting, swaggering.
Call me not cousin; each man for himself.
Some men are born to mirth and some to sorrow.   35
I am no cousin unto them that borrow.

                                        Exit TYDY

SUSAN

O Charity, why art thou fled to heaven,
And left all things on this earth uneven?
Their scoffing answers I will ne'er return,
But to myself his grief in silence mourn.   40

                        Enter SIR FRANCIS *and* MALBY

SIR FRANCIS

She is poor; I'll therefore tempt her with this gold.
Go, Malby, in my name deliver it,
And I will stay thy answer.

MALBY

Fair Mistress, as I understand, your grief
Doth grow from want, so I have here in store   45
A means to furnish you, a bag of gold
Which to your hands I freely tender you.

24 *flute* Q1 (Lute Q3)
32 *Cold comfort i.e.* discouraging; the phrase is proverbial
33 *roisting* revelling
38 *uneven* unequal, unjust
39 *return* either (a) report (to Charles) or (b) reply to, respond to
43 *stay* await
44 MALBY Q1 (*Fran.* Q3)
45 *in store* in plentiful supply

SUSAN
I thank you, heavens; I thank you, gentle sir!
God make me able to requite this favour.

MALBY
This gold Sir Francis Acton sends by me,   50
And prays you [*Whispers to her*]

SUSAN
Acton! O God, that name I am born to curse.
Hence bawd! hence broker! See, I spurn his gold;
My honour never shall for gain be sold.

SIR FRANCIS
Stay, lady, stay!

SUSAN   From you I'll posting hie,   55
Even as the doves from feathered eagles fly.

Exit SUSAN

SIR FRANCIS
She hates my name, my face; how should I woo?
I am disgraced in everything I do.
The more she hates me and disdains my love,
The more I am wrapped in admiration   60
Of her divine and chaste perfections.
Woo her with gifts I cannot, for all gifts
Sent in my name she spurns. With looks I cannot,
For she abhors my sight. Nor yet with letters,
For none she will receive. How then, how then?   65
Well I will fasten such a kindness on her
As shall o'ercome her hate and conquer it.
Sir Charles, her brother lies in execution
For a great sum of money, and besides,
The appeal is sued still for my huntsmen's death,   70
Which only I have power to reverse.
In her I'll bury all my hate of him.
Go seek the keeper, Malby, bring me to him.
To save his body, I his debts will pay;
To save his life, I his appeal will stay.   75

Exeunt SIR FRANCIS *and* MALBY

51 *prays you* Q3 (prayes you &c Q1) The *etcetera* has been taken to indicate stage
   business, in this case a whispered proposition. The instance of its use at Scene VI
   line 182 is different
55 *posting* in haste, hurriedly
68 *in execution* seized under legal enforcement, legally imprisoned
70 *appeal is sued still i.e.* he is still being pursued legally through the courts
70 *huntsmen's* Q3 (Huntsmans Q1)
73 *me to him* Q1 (him to me Q3)

SCENE X

Enter SIR CHARLES *in prison, with irons, his feet bare, his garments all ragged and torn*

SIR CHARLES
 Of all on the earth's face most miserable,
 Breathe in the hellish dungeon thy laments.
 Thus like a slave ragged, like a felon gyved,
 That hurls thee headlong to this base estate.
 O unkind uncle! O my friends ingrate!   5
 Unthankful kinsmen! Mountfords all too base!
 To let thy name lie fettered in disgrace!
 A thousand deaths here in this grave I die:
 Fear, hunger, sorrow, cold—all threat my death,
 And join together to deprive my breath.   10
 But that which most torments me, my dear sister
 Hath left to visit me, and from my friends
 Hath brought no hopeful answer; therefore I
 Divine they will not help my misery.
 If it be so, shame, scandal and contempt   15
 Attend their covetous thoughts, need make their graves.
 Usurers they live, and may they die like slaves.

Enter KEEPER

KEEPER
 Knight, be of comfort for I bring thee freedom
 From all thy troubles.

SIR CHARLES   Then I am doomed to die.
 Death is the end of all calamity.   20

KEEPER
 Live! Your appeal is stayed, the execution
 Of all your debts discharged, your creditors
 Even to the utmost penny satisfied,
 In sign whereof your shackles I knock off.
 You are not left so much indebted to us   25

 s.d. *feet* Q3 (*face* Q1)
 2 *the* Q1 (this Q3)
 3 *gyved* shackled
 5 *unkind* (a) unnatural or cruel (b) denying kinship
 5 *ingrate* ungrateful
 7 *lie* Q1 (be Q3)
 21 *stayed* stopped

As for your fees; all is discharged, all paid.
Go freely to your house, or where you please.
After long miseries, embrace your ease.

SIR CHARLES
Thou grumblest out the sweetest music to me
That ever organ played. Is this a dream?   30
Or do my waking senses apprehend
The pleasing taste of these applausive news?
Slave that I was to wrong such honest friends,
My loving kinsmen and my near allies.
Tongue, I will bite thee for the scandal breath   35
Against such faithful kinsmen. They are all
Composed of pity and compassion,
Of melting charity, and of moving ruth.
That which I spake before was in my rage;
They are my friends, the mirrors of this age,   40
Bounteous and free. The noble Mountfords' race
Ne'er bred a covetous thought or humour base.

Enter SUSAN

SUSAN
I can no longer stay from visiting
My woeful brother. While I could I kept
My hapless tidings from his hopeful ear.   45

SIR CHARLES
Sister, how much am I indebted to thee
And to thy travail.

SUSAN   What, at liberty?

SIR CHARLES
Thou seest I am, thanks to thy industry.
O unto which of all my courteous friends
Am I thus bound? My uncle Mountford? He   50
Even of an infant loved me; was it he?
So did my cousin Tydy; was it he?
So Master Roder, Master Sandy too;
Which of all these did this high kindness do?

---

32 *applausive* agreeable, acceptable
38 *ruth* compassion
40 *mirrors i.e.* models, exemplars
42 *humour* temperament, disposition
45 *hapless* unhappy, unfortunate (note the play on 'hopeful' later in the line)
47 *travail* trouble, exertion

SUSAN
Charles, can you mock me in your poverty,   55
Knowing your friends deride your misery.
Now I protest I stand so much amazed
To see your bonds free and your irons knocked off
That I am rapt into a maze of wonder,
The rather for I know not by what means   60
This happiness hath chanced.

SIR CHARLES   Why, by my uncle,
My cousins, and my friends; who else, I pray,
Would take upon them all my debts to pay?

SUSAN
O brother, they are men all of flint,
Pictures of marble, and as void of pity   65
As chased bears. I begged, I sued, I kneeled,
Laid open all your griefs and miseries,
Which they derided. More than that, denied us
A part in their alliance, but in pride
Said that our kindred with our plenty died.   70

SIR CHARLES
Drudges too much! What, did they? O known evil,
Rich fly the poor, as good men shun the Devil.
Whence should my freedom come; of whom alive,
Saving of those, have I deserved so well?
Guess, sister, call to mind, remember me.   75
These I have raised, these follow the world's guise,
Whom, rich in honour, they in woe despise.

SUSAN
My wits have lost themselves. Let's ask the keeper.

SIR CHARLES
Gaoler!

KEEPER
At hand, sir.   80

---

65 *Pictures of marble i.e.* statues
66 *chased* hunted, or possibly tormented (as in bear-baiting)
69 *alliance* kinship
71 *Drudges* slaves, servile creatures
76 *these* Q1 (they Q3)

---

77 *Whom... despise* an elliptical construction variously interpreted in its detail, but the
general sense is not in doubt: 'they despise you in misfortune, though you may be
rich in honour'

SIR CHARLES
    Of courtesy resolve me one demand:
    What was he took the burden of my debts
    From off my back, stayed my appeal to death,
    Discharged my fees, and brought me liberty?

KEEPER
    A courteous knight, one called Sir Francis Acton.   85

SUSAN
    Acton!

SIR CHARLES
    Ha! Acton! O me, more distressed in this
    Than all my troubles. Hale me back,
    Double my irons, and my sparing meals
    Put into halves, and lodge me in a dungeon   90
    More deep, more dark, more cold, more comfortless.
    By Acton freed! Not all thy manacles
    Could fetter so my heels as this one word
    Hath thralled my heart, and it must now lie bound
    In more strict prison than thy stony gaol.   95
    I am not free; I go but under bail.

KEEPER
    My charge is done, sir, now I have my fees.
    As we get little, we will nothing leese.   *Exit* KEEPER

SIR CHARLES
    By Acton freed, my dangerous opposite,
    Why? to what end? or what occasion? Ha!   100
    Let me forget the name of enemy,
    And with indifference balance this high favour. Ha!

SUSAN
    [*Aside*] His love to me, upon my soul 'tis so,
    That is the root from whence these strange things grow.

SIR CHARLES
    Had this proceeded from my father, he   105
    That by the law of nature is most bound

   85 *one* Q1 (and Q3)
   86 SUSAN *Acton!* Q1 (*omitted* Q3)
   92 *Acton* Q3 (action Q1)
   94 *thralled* brought into subjection, held captive
   98 *leese* lose, be deprived of
   99 *opposite* enemy, adversary
 100 *occasion* opportunity of taking advantage or attacking. *i.e.* 'What hold does it give
     him over me?'
 102 *indifference* impartiality
 102 *balance* weigh

In offices of love, it had deserved
My best employment to requite that grace.
Had it proceeded from my friends, or him,
From them this action had deserved my life,   110
And from a stranger more, because from such
There is less execution of good deeds.
But he, nor father, nor ally, nor friend,
More than a stranger, both remote in blood
And in his heart opposed my enemy,   115
That this high bounty should proceed from him!
O there I lose myself. What should I say?
What think? what do, his bounty to repay?

SUSAN
You wonder, I am sure, whence this strange kindness
Proceeds in Acton. I will tell you, brother.   120
He dotes on me, and oft hath sent me gifts,
Letters, and tokens: I refused them all.

SIR CHARLES
I have enough. Though poor, my heart is set
In one rich gift to pay back all my debt.

Exeunt SIR CHARLES *and* SUSAN

SCENE XI

Enter FRANKFORD *and* NICK, *with keys, and a letter in his hand*

FRANKFORD
This is the night, and I must play the touch
To try two seeming angels. Where's my keys?

NICK
They are made according to your mould in wax.

---

108 *employment* endeavours
109 *him i.e.* from my father
112 *execution* performance
  1 *and* Q1 (that Q3)
  1 *the touch* Q1 (my part Q3)
  1-2 *touch... angels i.e.* metaphorically test the worth of two apparently current coins
      by using a touchstone. There is of course a pun on 'angels'

---

119 *strange kindness* The phrase is paradoxical in a way closely related to the central
    paradox of the play
    s.d. *with keys, and a letter in his hand* Q1, Q3. It is not entirely clear who has the
    letter; lines 5-6 suggest that it is Frankford who carries it onto the stage. But the
    alternative is not at all impossible, so I have left the text as it stands in the quartos

I bade the smith be secret, gave him money,
And there they are. The letter, sir.   5

FRANKFORD
True, take it; there it is.
And when thou seest me in my pleasant'st vein
Ready to sit to supper, bring it me.

NICK
I'll do't, make no more question but I'll do't.

Exit NICK

Enter ANNE, CRANWELL, WENDOLL *and* JENKIN

ANNE
Sirrah, 'tis six o'clock already struck.   10
Go bid them spread the cloth and serve in supper.

JENKIN
It shall be done forsooth, mistress. Where is Spiggot the
butler to give us out salt and trenchers?

WENDOLL
We that have been ahunting all the day
Come with prepared stomachs, Master Frankford.   15
We wished you at our sport.

FRANKFORD
My heart was with you, and my mind was on you.
Fie, Master Cranwell, you are still thus sad.
A stool, a stool! Where's Jenkin, and where's Nick?
'Tis supper time at least an hour ago.   20
What's the best news abroad?

WENDOLL   I know none good.

FRANKFORD
[*Aside*] But I know too much bad.

Enter SPIGGOT *and* JENKIN *with a tablecloth, bread, trenchers, and
salt* [*, then exeunt*]

CRANWELL
Methinks, sir, you might have that interest
In your wife's brother to be more remiss

5 *there* Q1 (heere Q3)
5 *The letter, sir.* Q3 (*Erroneously given as a separate speech by Nick in Q1*)
7 *pleasant'st* ed. (pleasantst Q1; pleasants Q3)
13 *out* Q1 (our Q3)
13 *trenchers* plates
15 *with prepared stomachs i.e.* with good appetites
23 *interest* Q3 (intrest Q1) *i.e.* influence (over or with)
24 *more remiss* less strict, more lenient

In this hard dealing against poor Sir Charles,   25
Who, as I hear, lies in York Castle, needy
And in great want.

FRANKFORD
Did not more weighty business of my own
Hold me away, I would have laboured peace
Betwixt them with all care; indeed I would, sir.   30

ANNE
I'll write unto my brother earnestly
In that behalf.

WENDOLL   A charitable deed,
And will beget the good opinion
Of all your friends that love you, Mistress Frankford.

FRANKFORD
That's you for one; I know you love Sir Charles   35
[*Aside*] And my wife too well.

WENDOLL   He deserves the love
Of all true gentlemen. Be yourselves judge.

FRANKFORD
But supper, ho! Now as thou lovest me, Wendoll,
Which I am sure thou dost, be merry, pleasant,
And frolic it tonight. Sweet Master Cranwell,   40
Do you the like. Wife, I protest my heart
Was ne'er more bent on sweet alacrity.
Where be those lazy knaves to serve in supper?

Enter NICK

NICK
Sir, here's a letter.

FRANKFORD
Whence comes it? and who brought it?   45

NICK
A stripling that below attends your answer,
And as he tells me it is sent from York.

25 *this* Q1 (his Q3)
25 *dealing* conduct, behaviour
28 *my* Q1 (mine Q3)
34 *Mistress* Q3 (Master Q1)
42 *alacrity* lively enjoyment
44 *Sir, here's a letter* Q1 (Here's a letter sir Q3)

FRANKFORD
   Have him into the cellar; let him taste
   A cup of our March beer. Go, make him drink. [*Reads*]
NICK
   I'll make him drunk, if he be a Trojan.   [*Exit*]   50
FRANKFORD
   My boots and spurs! Where's Jenkin? God forgive me,
   How I neglect my business. Wife, look here,
   I have a matter to be tried tomorrow
   By eight o'clock, and my attorney writes me
   I must be there betimes with evidence,   55
   Or it will go against me. Where's my boots?

              Enter JENKIN *with boots and spurs*

ANNE
   I hope your business craves no such dispatch
   That you must ride tonight.
WENDOLL [*Aside*]   I hope it doth.
FRANKFORD
   God's me! No such dispatch?
   Jenkin, my boots. Where's Nick? Saddle my roan,   60
   And the grey dapple for himself.   [*Exit* JENKIN]
                              Content ye,
   It much concerns me. Gentle Master Cranwell
   And Master Wendoll, in my absence use
   The very ripest pleasure of my house.
WENDOLL
   Lord, Master Frankford, will you ride tonight?   65
   The ways are dangerous.
FRANKFORD   Therefore will I ride
   Appointed well, and so shall Nick, my man.

48–9 *Lineation* ed. (Have...cup/Of...drink Q1; *as prose* Q3)
50 *Trojan* the colloquial sense is 'a roisterer, one who leads a dissolute life, a good
   fellow'. Following Bates, Van Fossen cites Heywood's use of the term in
   Philocothista (1635) for 'drunkard'
51–2 *Lineation* Q1 (*as prose* Q3)
51 *where's* Q3 (whetes Q1)
55 *betimes* early in the morning
59 *God's me* i.e. God save me
61 *Content ye* Be assured
66 *ways are dangerous* a reference to the footpads and highwaymen that constituted a
   threat to travellers in the period
67 *Appointed well* well armed

ANNE
  I'll call you up by five o'clock tomorrow.

FRANKFORD
  No, by my faith, wife, I'll not trust to that.
  'Tis not such easy rising in a morning   70
  From one I love so dearly. No, by my faith,
  I shall not leave so sweet a bedfellow
  But with much pain. You have made me a sluggard
  Since I first knew you.

ANNE   Then if you needs will go
  This dangerous evening, Master Wendoll,   75
  Let me entreat you bear him company.

WENDOLL
  With all my heart, sweet mistress. My boots there!

FRANKFORD
  Fie, fie, that for my private business
  I should disease my friend, and be a trouble
  To the whole house. Nick!   80

                [*Enter* NICK]

NICK
  Anon, sir.

FRANKFORD
  Bring forth my gelding.   [*Exit* NICK]
                As you love me, sir,
  Use no more words. A hand, good Master Cranwell.

CRANWELL
  Sir, God be your good speed.

FRANKFORD
  Goodnight, sweet Nan. Nay, nay, a kiss and part. 85
  [*Aside*] Dissembling lips, you suit not with my heart.

                        Exit FRANKFORD

WENDOLL
  [*Aside*] How business, time and hours all gracious proves,
  And are the furtherers to my new born love.
  I am husband now in Master Frankford's place,
  And must command the house. [*To* ANNE] My pleasure is 90
  We will not sup abroad so publicly,
  But in your private chamber, Mistress Frankford.

79 *disease* disturb, inconvenience
86 *suit not* do not match
87 *proves* Q1 (proue Q3)

ANNE
  [*To* WENDOLL] O sir, you are too public in your love,
  And Master Frankford's wife—

CRANWELL   Might I crave favour,
  I would entreat you I might see my chamber.   95
  I am on the sudden grown exceeding ill,
  And would be spared from supper.

WENDOLL   Light there, ho!
  See you want nothing, sir, for if you do
  You injure that good man, and wrong me too.

CRANWELL
  I will make bold. Goodnight.   *Exit* CRANWELL

WENDOLL   How all conspire   100
  To make our bosom sweet and full entire.
  Come, Nan, I prithee let us sup within.

ANNE
  O what a clog unto the soul is sin.
  We pale offenders are, still full of fear;
  Every suspicious eye brings danger near,   105
  When they whose clear heart from offence are free
  Despise report, base scandals do outface,
  And stand at mere defiance with disgrace.

WENDOLL
  Fie, fie, you talk too like a puritan.

ANNE
  You have tempted me to mischief, Master Wendoll.   110
  I have done I know not what. Well, you plead custom;
  That which for want of wit I granted erst

---

   99 *injure* Q3 (injury Q1) The two forms were synonymous, though *c*1600 'injury' was
      supplanted as a verb by the current form. The compositors' preferences may simply
      record this process
  101 *bosom* desires (cf. *Measure for Measure* IV.iii, 139 'You shall have your bosom on
      this fellow.') Van Fossen defines it as 'intimacy'
  103 *clog* impediment, encumbrance (see I.58 above)
  104 *pale i.e.* pale from fear, timorous
  106 *When* while, whereas
  107 *do* Q3 (to Q1)
  109 *puritan* Q3 (Puritant Q1) Whether Q1's is a variant form or a variant spelling is not
      clear, though *OED* records it and suggests that it was formed by analogy with
      'protestant'
  111 *plead custom i.e.* that sin has acquired the force of right by habitual practice (an
      allusion to the legal force of custom)
  112 *erst* first

I now must yield through fear. Come, come, let's in.
Once o'er shoes, we are straight o'er head in sin.

WENDOLL

My jocund soul is joyful above measure;   115
I'll be profuse in Frankford's richest treasure.

Exeunt

SCENE XII

Enter SISLY, JENKIN and SPIGGOT

JENKIN

My mistress and Master Wendoll, my master, sup in her
chamber tonight. Sisly, you are preferred from being the
cook to be chambermaid. Of all the loves betwixt thee and
me, tell me what thou thinkest of this.

SISLY

Mum; there's an old proverb, 'When the cat's away, the   5
mouse may play'.

JENKIN

Now you talk of a cat, Sisly, I smell a rat.

SISLY

Good words, Jenkin, lest you be called to answer them.

JENKIN

Why, God make my mistress an honest woman—are not
these good words? Pray God my new master play not the   10
knave with my old master—is there any hurt in this? God
send no villainy intended, and if they do sup together,
pray God they do not lie together. God keep my mistress
chaste, and make us all His servants—what harm is there
in all this? Nay, more: here is my hand; thou shalt never   15
have my heart unless thou say 'Amen'.

2 *preferred* promoted
5 *Mum* be silent
8 *Good words i.e.* be careful what you say
13 *keep* Q1 (make Q3)

s.d. *and* SPIGGOT ed. (and Butler Q3; Butler, and other Seruingmen Q1) Given the
entry at line 17, and the nature of Jenkin's remarks, the entry of servingmen at this
point seems unlikely. I have therefore followed Q3

SISLY
Amen, I pray God, I say.

Enter SERVINGMEN

SERVINGMAN
My mistress sends that you should make less noise, to
lock up the doors, and see the household all got to bed.
You, Jenkin, for this night are made the porter, to see the   20
gates shut in.

JENKIN
Thus, by little and little, I creep into office. Come, to
kennel, my masters, to kennel; 'tis eleven o'clock already.

SERVINGMAN
When you have locked the gates in, you must send up the
keys to my mistress.   25

SISLY
Quickly, for God's sake, Jenkin, for I must carry them. I
am neither pillow nor bolster, but I know more than both.

JENKIN
To bed, good Spiggot; to bed, good honest serving
creatures, and let us sleep as snug as pigs in pease-straw.

Exeunt

SCENE XIII

Enter FRANKFORD *and* NICK

FRANKFORD
Soft, soft. We have tied our geldings to a tree
Two flight shoot off, lest by their thundering hooves
They blab our coming back. Hearest thou no noise?

20 *this* Q3 (*his* Q1, *but with catchword reading* 'this')
23 *to kennel* i.e. as though they were a pack of hounds
29 *pease-straw* straw from the pea plant. The phrase 'as snug as pigs in pease-straw' is
  proverbial
1 *our* Q1 (*your* Q3)
1-3 *As prose in quartos*
2 *two flight shoot* flight-shot arrows were specifically designed for distance competi-
  tions, so here, a distance twice the maximum range of bow and arrow
3 *blab* betray, reveal
3 *back* Q1 (*omitted* Q3)

---

17 SERVINGMEN Q1, Q3. See above. The stage business at this point requires only one
  servant, who comes on as a messenger, but the quartos agree on a plural. (This
  may, of course, be an instance of Q3's dependence on Q1.)

NICK
    Hear? I hear nothing but the owl and you.

FRANKFORD
    So; now my watch's hand points upon twelve,   5
    And it is dead midnight. Where are my keys?

NICK
    Here, sir.

FRANKFORD
    This is the key that opes my outward gate;
    This is the hall door; this my withdrawing chamber.
    But this, that door that's bawd unto my shame,   10
    Fountain and spring of all my bleeding thoughts,
    Where the most hallowed order and true knot
    Of nuptial sanctity hath been profaned.
    It leads to my polluted bed-chamber,
    Once my terrestial heaven, now my earth's hell,   15
    The place where sins in all their ripeness dwell.
    But I forget myself; now to my gate.

NICK
    It must ope with far less noise than Cripplegate, or your
    plot's dashed.

FRANKFORD
    So, reach me my dark lantern to the rest.   20
    Tread softly, softly.

NICK
    I will walk on eggs this pace.

FRANKFORD
    A general silence hath surprised the house,
    And this is the last door. Astonishment,
    Fear and amazement play against my heart,   25
    Even as a madman beats upon a drum.

4 Hear? Q1 (omitted Q3)
6 dead Q1 (iust Q3)
9 is Q1 (omitted Q3)
9 my Q1 (the Q3)
9 withdrawing chamber a room to withdraw to, now a drawing room
20 dark lantern a lantern having an arrangement by which the light could be concealed
22 walk on eggs this pace i.e. 'I'm treading so softly I could walk on eggs.'
23 surprised overtaken
25 play against Q1 (beate vpon Q3)

18 Cripplegate one of the gates to the old city of London. If the play was performed at
    the Red Bull theatre (as seems likely) this would be the gate through which
    spectators passed en route to the playhouse

O keep my eyes, you heavens, before I enter,
From any sight that may transfix my soul.
Or if there be so black a spectacle,
O strike mine eyes stark blind; or if not so,   30
Lend me such patience to digest my grief
That I may keep this white and virgin hand
From any violent outrage or red murder.
And with that prayer I enter.   [*Exit* FRANKFORD]

NICK
[*Aside*] Here's a circumstance!   35
A man may be made cuckold in the time
That he's about it. And the case were mine,
As 'tis my master's,—'sblood that he makes me swear—
I would have placed his action, entered there.
I would, I would.   40

            [*Enter* FRANKFORD]

FRANKFORD
O, O!

NICK
Master, 'sblood, master, master!

FRANKFORD
O me unhappy! I have found them lying
Close in each other's arms, and fast asleep.
But that I would not damn two precious souls   45
Bought with my Saviour's blood, and send them laden
With all their scarlet sins upon their backs
Unto a fearful judgement, their two lives
Had met upon my rapier.

NICK
'Sblood, master, have you left them sleeping still?   50
Let me go wake them.

35-8 *Lineation* Q1 (*as prose* Q3)
35 *circumstance* Q1 (circumstance indeed Q3)
36 *cuckold* Q1 (a Cuckold Q3)
37 *That* Q1 (*omitted* Q3)
37 *And* if
44 *other's* Q1 (other Q3)
50-1 *Lineation* Q3 (*as prose* Q1)
50 *'Sblood, master* Q1 (Master what Q3)
51 *them* Q1 (em Q3)

---

39 *placed his action* It is unclear whether 'his' refers to Frankford or to Wendoll. The
phrase could mean 'determined what Wendoll was doing' or 'established
Frankford's case (against Wendoll)'

FRANKFORD
   Stay; let me pause awhile.
   O God, O God, that it were possible
   To undo things done, to call back yesterday;
   That Time could turn up his swift sandy glass   55
   To untell the days, and to redeem these hours.
   Or that the sun
   Could, rising from the west, draw his coach backward,
   Take from the acount of Time so many minutes,
   Till he had all these seasons called again,   60
   Those minutes and those actions done in them,
   Even from her first offence, that I might take her
   As spotless as an angel in my arms.
   But O! I talk of things impossible,
   And cast beyond the moon. God give me patience,   65
   For I will in to wake them.   *Exit* FRANKFORD

NICK
   Here's patience perforce!
   He needs must trot afoot that tires his horse.

     Enter WENDOLL *running over the stage in a nightgown,*
     [FRANKFORD] *after him with his sword drawn; the maid in her*
     smock stays his hand and clasps hold on him; he pauses awhile

FRANKFORD
   I thank thee, maid. Thou like the angel's hand
   Hath stayed me from a bloody sacrifice.   70
   Go, villain, and my wrongs sit on thy soul
   As heavy as this grief doth upon mine.
   When thou recordest my many courtesies
   And shalt compare them with thy treacherous heart,
   Lay them together, weigh them equally,   75
   'Twill be revenge enough. Go, to thy friend
   A Judas. Pray, pray, lest I live to see
   Thee Judas-like hanged on an elder tree.

     Enter ANNE *in her smock, nightgown and night attire*

55 *sandy glass i.e.* an hourglass filled with sand
56 *to untell i.e.* to count backwards in time
66 *to* Q1 (and Q3)
67 *perforce* of necessity. The phrase is proverbial
69 *the* Q1 (an Q3)
74 *shalt* Q1 (shall Q3)

69-70 *angel's hand...sacrifice* The reference is to Abraham's proposed sacrifice of
    Issac, in *Genesis* xii, 11-12
78 *hanged on an elder tree* it was traditionally believed that the tree on which Judas
    hanged himself was an elder. See Note on VIII.106 above, and Introduction

ANNE

O by what word, what title, or what name
Shall I entreat your pardon? Pardon! O   80
I am as far from hoping such sweet grace
As Lucifer from heaven. To call you husband!
O me most wretched, I have lost that name;
I am no more your wife.

NICK   'Sblood, sir, she sounds.

FRANKFORD

Spare thou thy tears, for I will weep for thee;   85
And keep thy countenance, for I'll blush for thee.
Now I protest, I think 'tis I am tainted,
For I am most ashamed, and 'tis more hard
For me to look upon thy guilty face
Than on the sun's clear brow. What wouldst thou speak?   90

ANNE

I would I had no tongue, no ears, no eyes,
No apprehension, no capacity.
When do you spurn me like a dog? When tread me
Under your feet? When drag me by the hair?
Though I deserve a thousand thousandfold   95
More than you can inflict, yet, once my husband,
For womanhood—to which I am a shame
Though once an ornament—even for His sake
That hath redeemed our souls, mark not my face
Nor hack me with your sword, but let me go   100
Perfect and undeformed to my tomb.
I am not worthy that I should prevail
In the least suit, no, not to speak to you,
Nor look on you, nor to be in your presence.
Yet, as an abject, this one suit I crave;   105
This granted, I am ready for my grave.

FRANKFORD

My God with patience arm me! Rise, nay, rise,
And I'll debate with thee. Was it for want
Thou playedst the strumpet? Wast thou not supplied

---

84 *sounds* i.e. swoons, faints
90 *What...speak?* Q1 (*a separate line in* Q3)
94 *your feet* Q1 (feete Q3)
97 *a shame* ed. (ashamd Q1; asham'd Q3) Dodsley's suggested emendation supplies a
   grammatical parallel with 'ornament'
105 *an abject* one who has been cast aside

With every pleasure, fashion, and new toy,   110
Nay, even beyond my calling?

ANNE   I was.

FRANKFORD
Was it then disability in me,
Or in thine eye seemed he a properer man?

ANNE
O no.

FRANKFORD   Did I not lodge thee in my bosom?
Wear thee here in my heart?

ANNE   You did.   115

FRANKFORD
I did indeed; witness my tears I did.
Go bring my infants hither.

          [*Exit* MAID. *Enter* MAID *again with* TWO CHILDREN]
                          O Nan, O Nan,
If neither fear of shame, regard of honour,
The blemish of my house, nor my dear love
Could have withheld thee from so lewd a fact,   120
Yet for these infants, these young harmless souls,
On whose white brows thy shame is charactered,
And grows in greatness as they wax in years,
Look but on them, and melt away in tears.
Away with them, lest as her spotted body   125

---

113 *properer* handsomer
114–15 *Lineation* Q3 (Did I...thee/Here in my hart. Q1)
114 *I not* Q1 (not I Q3)
114 *my* Q3 (thy Q1)
115 *here in* Q1 (in Q3)
118 *neither* Q3 (either Q1)
120 *fact* action, deed
122 *charactered* imprinted, written
123 *wax* grow
125 *spotted* morally stained

---

111 *beyond my calling* Van Fossen glosses calling as 'rank, station in life', with the
    implication, presumably, that he had over-indulged her whims. But the word also
    has the sense of 'duty, that which is morally or religiously required of one'. The
    distinction is an interesting one for readers scrutinizing the Frankfords'
    relationship

Hath stained their names with stripe of bastardy,
So her adulterous breath may blast their spirits
With her infectious thoughts. Away with them!

[Exeunt MAID *with* CHILDREN]

ANNE
In this one life I die ten thousand deaths.

FRANKFORD
Stand up, stand up. I will do nothing rashly.   130
I will retire awhile into my study,
And thou shalt hear thy sentence presently.

Exit FRANKFORD

ANNE
'Tis welcome, be it death. O me, base strumpet,
That having such a husband, such sweet children,
Must enjoy neither. O to redeem my honour   135
I would have this hand cut off, these my breasts seared,
Be racked, strappadoed, put to any torment.
Nay, to whip but this scandal out, I would hazard
The rich and dear redemption of my soul.
He cannot be so base as to forgive me,   140
Nor I so shameless to accept his pardon.
O women, women, you that have yet kept
Your holy matrimonial vow unstained,
Make me your instance: when you tread awry,
Your sins like mine will on your conscience lie.   145

Enter SISLY, SPIGGOT, *all the* SERVINGMEN *and* JENKIN,
as newly come out of bed

ALL
O mistress, mistress, what have you done, mistress?

127 *blast* blight
132 *presently* immediately, in a very short space of time
135 *my* Q1 (mine Q3)
136 *seared i.e.* with hot irons
137 *strappadoed* a horrendous punishment or torture in which the arms were fastened
    behind the back and the victim hoisted by them into the air until he was his own
    height above the ground. He was then allowed to drop halfway down and his fall
    arrested with a jerk
142 *have yet* Q1 (yet haue Q3)
144 *instance* example, lesson

126 *stripe of bastardy* This example is cited by the *OED* as a figurative use of the *stripe*
    left by the rod of punishment, therefore a badge of shame, in this case of
    illegitimacy. Van Fossen draws attention to the heraldic use of the bend sinister to
    denote bastardy in arms

NICK
  'Sblood, what a caterwauling keep you here.

JENKIN
  O Lord, mistress, how comes this to pass? My master is
  run away in his shirt, and never so much as called me to
  bring his clothes after him.   150

ANNE
  See what guilt is: here stand I in this place,
  Ashamed to look my servants in the face.

  Enter MASTER FRANKFORD *and* CRANWELL, *whom seeing*
  she falls on her knees

FRANKFORD
  My words are registered in heaven already;
  With patience hear me. I'll not martyr thee,
  Nor mark thee for a strumpet, but with usage   155
  Of more humility torment thy soul,
  And kill thee, even with kindness.

CRANWELL   Master Frankford—

FRANKFORD
  Good Master Cranwell—woman, hear thy judgement:
  Go, make thee ready in thy best attire,
  Take with thee all thy gowns, all thy apparel;   160
  Leave nothing that did ever call thee mistress,
  Or by whose sight being left here in the house
  I may remember such a woman by.
  Choose thee a bed and hangings for a chamber;
  Take with thee everything that hath thy mark,   165
  And get thee to my manor seven mile off,
  Where live. 'Tis thine; I freely give it thee.
  My tenants by shall furnish thee with wains
  To carry all thy stuff, within two hours,
  No longer, will I limit thee my sight.   170
  Choose which of all my servants thou likest best,
  And they are thine to attend thee.

ANNE   A mild sentence.

147 *'Sblood, what* Q1 (VVhat Q3)
147 *caterwauling* a noise like that of cats in heat
149 *shirt* nightshirt
164 *a chamber* Q1 (thy chamber Q3)
165 *that* Q1 (which Q3)
168 *wains* wagons
170 *will I limit thee my sight i.e.* will I permit you to remain within my sight

FRANKFORD

But, as thou hopest for heaven, as thou believest
Thy name's recorded in the book of life,
I charge thee never after this sad day   175
To see me, or to meet me, or to send
By word, or writing, gift, or otherwise
To move me, by thyself, or by thy friends,
Nor challenge any part in my two children.
So farewell, Nan, for we will henceforth be   180
As we had never seen, ne'er more shall see.

ANNE

How full my heart is in my eyes appears.
What wants in words, I will supply in tears.

FRANKFORD

Come, take your coach, your stuff; all must along.
Servants and all make ready, all be gone.   185
It was thy hand cut two hearts out of one.

                                                        [*Exeunt*]

SCENE XIV

Enter SIR CHARLES, *gentlemanlike, and* [SUSAN] *his sister,
gentlewomanlike*

SUSAN

Brother, why have you tricked me like a bride?
Bought me this gay attire, these ornaments?
Forget you our estate, our poverty?

SIR CHARLES

Call me not brother, but imagine me
Some barbarous outlaw, or uncivil kerne,   5
For if thou shutt'st thy eye, and only hearest
The words that I shall utter, thou shalt judge me
Some staring ruffian, not thy brother Charles.
O Susan!

---

174 *book of life* in the Bible the book containing the names of those who will inherit
    eternal life
182 *my eyes* Q1 (mine eies Q3)
  1 *tricked* dressed, adorned, decked
  3 *estate i.e.* financial circumstances
  5 *uncivil kerne* uncivilised peasant or boor
  8 *staring* wild, frantic
  8 *ruffian* Q3 (Ruffin Q1)

SUSAN
  O brother, what doth this strange language mean?   10

SIR CHARLES
  Dost love me, sister? Wouldst thou see me live
  A bankrupt beggar in the world's disgrace,
  And die indebted to my enemies?
  Wouldst thou behold me stand like a huge beam
  In the world's eye, a byword and a scorn?   15
  It lies in thee of these to acquit me free,
  And all my debt I may outstrip by thee.

SUSAN
  By me? Why I have nothing, nothing left;
  I owe even for the clothes upon my back.
  I am not worth—

SIR CHARLES   O sister, say not so.   20
  It lies in you my downcast state to raise,
  To make me stand on even points with the world.
  Come, sister, you are rich! Indeed you are!
  And in your power you have, without delay,
  Acton's five hundred pound back to repay.   25

SUSAN
  Till now I had thought you loved me, by mine honour,
  Which I had kept as spotless as the moon.
  I ne'er was mistress of that single doit
  Which I reserved not to supply your wants,
  And do you think that I would hoard from you?   30
  Now, by my hopes in heaven, knew I the means
  To buy you from the slavery of your debts,
  Especially from Acton, whom I hate,
  I would redeem it with my life or blood.

---

13 *my* Q1 (mine Q3)
14–15 *beam/ In the world's eye* i.e. in conspicuous disgrace. The allusion is to the well-known figure used in the Sermon on the Mount (*Matthew*, vii. 3) of the mote and the beam
15 *byword* object of scorn and contempt
20 *worth*—ed. (worth, &c Q1; worth Q3) The ampersand in Q1 seems here to indicate interruption. (Cf. the use of the etcetera at VI. 182, and, IX. 51 note)
22 *even points* equal terms
26 *you loved* Q1 (y'had lou'd Q3)
26 *mine* Q1 (my Q3)
27 *had* Q1 (haue Q3)
28 *doit* originally a Dutch coin of very slight value, it came to stand as the type of a small amount
30 *do you* Q1 (de'ye Q3)

SIR CHARLES
> I challenge it, and, kindred set apart,   35
> Thus ruffianlike I lay seige to your heart:
> What do I owe to Acton?

SUSAN
> Why, some five hundred pounds, toward which I swear
> In all the world I have not one denier.

SIR CHARLES
> It will not prove so, sister. Now resolve me: 40
> What do you think—and speak your conscience—
> Would Acton give might he enjoy your bed?

SUSAN
> He would not shrink to spend a thousand pound
> To give the Mountford's name so deep a wound.

SIR CHARLES
> A thousand pound! I but five hundred owe;   45
> Grant him your bed, he's paid with interest so.

SUSAN
> O brother!

SIR CHARLES O sister! Only this one way,
> With that rich jewel, you my debts may pay.
> In speaking this my cold heart shakes with shame,
> Nor do I woo you in a brother's name,   50
> But in a stranger's. Shall I die in debt
> To Acton, my grand foe, and you still wear
> The precious jewel that he holds so dear?

SUSAN
> My honour I esteem as dear and precious
> As my redemption.

SIR CHARLES   I esteem you, sister,   55
> As dear for so dear prizing it.

SUSAN   Will Charles
> Have me cut off my hands, and send them Acton?
> Rip up my breast, and with my bleeding heart
> Present him as a token.

36 *your* Q1 (*thy* Q3)

38 *toward which I swear* Q1 (*separate line* Q3)

39 *denier* like *doit* (above 1.28) used as the type of a very small sum of money, originally a small French coin worth one twelfth of a sou

41 *conscience i.e.* what you know inwardly (without the moral sense of the present-day meaning)

55–6 *I esteem ... sister,/As ... it.* Q1 (I esteem ... deare,/For so prizing it. Q3)

59 *token* present, keepsake

SIR CHARLES   Neither, sister,
  But hear me in my strange assertion: 60
  Thy honour and my soul are equal in my regard,
  Nor will thy brother Charles survive thy shame.
  His kindness like a burden hath surcharged me,
  And under his good deeds I stooping go,
  Not with an upright soul. Had I remained   65
  In prison still, there doubtless I had died.
  Then unto him that freed me from that prison
  Still do I owe that life. What moved my foe
  To enfranchise me? 'Twas, sister, for your love.
  With full five hundred pounds he bought your love,   70
  And shall he not enjoy it? Shall the weight
  Of all this heavy burden lean on me,
  And will not you bear part? You did partake
  The joy of my release; will you not stand
  In joint bond bound to satisfy the debt?   75
  Shall I be only charged?

SUSAN   But that I know
  These arguments come from an honoured mind,
  As in your most extremity of need,
  Scorning to stand in debt to one you hate,
  Nay, rather would engage your unstained honour   80
  Than to be held ingrate, I should condemn you.
  I see your resolution and assent;
  So Charles will have me, and I am content.

SIR CHARLES
  For this I tricked you up.

SUSAN   But here's a knife,
  To save mine honour, shall slice out my life.   85

SIR CHARLES
  I know thou pleasest me a thousand times
  More in that resolution than thy grant.
  [*Aside*] Observe her love; to soothe them in my suit
  Her honour she will hazard, though not lose.
  To bring me out of debt, her rigorous hand   90

59 *sister* Q3 (Iane Q1)
63 *surcharged* overburdened, overloaded
69 *enfranchise* free, release from gaol
80 *engage* expose to risk, compromise
87 *that* Q1 (thy Q3)
88 *them in* Q1 (it to Q3)
88 *to soothe them in my suit* to appease those who are pursuing me

Will pierce her heart. O wonder, that will choose
Rather than stain her blood, her life to lose.
[*To her*] Come, you sad sister to a woeful brother,
This is the gate. I'll bear him such a present,
Such an acquittance for the knight to seal,   95
As will amaze his senses, and surprise
With admiration all his fantasies.

Enter ACTON *and* MALBY

SUSAN
Before his unchaste thoughts shall seize on me
'Tis here shall my imprisoned soul set free.

SIR FRANCIS
How! Mountford with his sister hand in hand!   100
What miracle's afoot?

MALBY   It is a sight
Begets in me much admiration.

SIR CHARLES
Stand not amazed to see me thus attended.
Acton, I owe thee money, and being unable
To bring thee the full sum in ready coin,   105
Lo! for thy more assurance here's a pawn,
My sister, my dear sister, whose chaste honour
I prize above a million. Here, nay, take her;
She's worth your money, man; do not forsake her.

SIR FRANCIS
[*Aside*] I would he were in earnest.   110

SUSAN
Impute it not to my immodesty.
My brother being rich in nothing else
But in his interest that he hath in me,
According to his poverty hath brought you
Me, all his store, whom howsoe'er you prize   115
As forfeit to your hand, he values highly,
And would not sell but to acquit your debt
For any emperor's ransom.

---

95 *acquittance... to seal* document discharging the debt for Sir Francis to sign with his
   seal
97 *admiration* astonishment, wonder
99 *'Tis here i.e.* the knife which will release her
106 *pawn i.e.* a pledge of security for the debt (*see* I.96)
113 *interest* a pun on the emotional and financial senses of the word

SIR FRANCIS [*Aside*]   Stern heart, relent;
 Thy former cruelty at length repent.
 Was ever known in any former age   120
 Such honourable wrested courtesy?
 Lands, honours, lives, and all the world forgo
 Rather than stand engaged to such a foe.

SIR CHARLES
 Acton, she is too poor to be thy bride,
 And I too much opposed to be thy brother.   125
 There, take her to thee; if thou hast the heart
 To seize her as a rape or lustful prey,
 To blur our house that never yet was stained,
 To murder her that never meant thee harm,
 To kill me now whom once thou savedst from death,   130
 Do them at once on her; all these rely
 And perish with her spotted chastity.

SIR FRANCIS
 You overcome me in your love, Sir Charles.
 I cannot be so cruel to a lady
 I love so dearly. Since you have not spared   135
 To engage your reputation to the world,
 Your sister's honour which you prize so dear,
 Nay, all the comforts which you hold on earth,
 To grow out of my debt, being your foe,
 Your honoured thoughts, lo, thus I recompence: 140
 Your metamorphised foe receives your gift
 In satisfaction of all former wrongs.
 This jewel I will wear here in my heart,
 And where before I thought her for her wants
 Too base to be my bride, to end all strife   145
 I seal you my dear brother, her my wife.

121 *wrested* strained, distorted
122 *lives* Q1 (life Q3)
127 *lustful prey* victim of your lust
128 *blur* blemish, defile
131 *at once i.e.* in one action, since all of these consequences depend upon how you treat
    her
131 *rely i.e.* rely upon, depend upon
138 *comforts* Q1 (comfort Q3)
139 *To grow out of i.e.* in order to grow out of, to disburden yourself
144 *her wants i.e.* her poverty and lack of status

146 *seal* It may be noted that Acton here and in his use of the word 'jewel' above (line
    143) now echoes the language employed earlier by Sir Charles (see line 95 and
    47–53)

SUSAN
    You still exceed us. I will yield to fate
    And learn to love where I till now did hate.

SIR CHARLES
    With that enchantment you have charmed my soul,
    And made me rich even in those very words.   150
    I pay no debt but am indebted more;
    Rich in your love I never can be poor.

SIR FRANCIS
    All's mine is yours; we are alike in state.
    Let's knit in love what was opposed in hate.
    Come, for our nuptials we will straight provide,   155
    Blest only in our brother and fair bride.

                                        Exeunt

SCENE XV

Enter CRANWELL, FRANKFORD *and* NICK

CRANWELL
    Why do you search each room about your house,
    Now that you have dispatched your wife away?

FRANKFORD
    O sir, to see that nothing may be left
    That ever was my wife's. I loved her dearly,
    And when I do but think of her unkindness,   5
    My thoughts are all in hell, to avoid which torment,
    I would not have a bodkin or a cuff,
    A bracelet, necklace, or rebato wire,
    Nor anything that ever was called hers
    Left me, by which I might remember her.   10
    Seek round about.

153 *All's* Q3 (Alas Q1)
156 *Blest only i.e.* without (the blessing of) a dowry
    7 *bodkin* a long pin used to fasten up the hair
    7 *cuff i.e.* an ornamental cuff
    8 *rebato wire* collar made of wire to support a ruff in the dress of the period
    9 *called* Q3 (*omitted* Q1)

150–52 *And made...poor* This passage signals the completion of one of the thematic
    discussions carried forward by the play, that of the value and significance of wealth
    as source of honour. The mismatch is resolved by love, whereas even moments
    before they were still perceiving one another's action in terms of 'exceed' (147) and
    'overcome' (133). Now Sir Francis can observe 'we are alike in state'

NICK
  'Sblood, master, here's her lute flung in a corner.

FRANKFORD
  Her lute! O God, upon this instrument
  Her fingers have run quick division,
  Sweeter than that which now divides our hearts.   15
  These frets have made me pleasant, that have now
  Frets of my heartstrings made. O Master Cranwell,
  Oft hath she made this melancholy wood,
  Now mute and dumb for her disastrous chance,
  Speak sweetly many a note, sound many a strain   20
  To her own ravishing voice, which being well strung,
  What pleasant strange airs have they jointly sung.
  Post with it after her. Now nothing's left;
  Of her and hers I am at once bereft.

NICK
  I'll ride and overtake her, do my message,   25
  And come back again.   [*Exit* NICK]
CRANWELL   Meantime, sir, if you please,
  I'll to Sir Francis Acton and inform him
  Of what hath passed betwixt you and his sister.

FRANKFORD
  Do as you please. How ill am I bestead
  To be a widower ere my wife be dead.   30

                [*Exeunt* FRANKFORD *and* CRANWELL]

SCENE XVI

Enter ANNE, *with* JENKIN, *her maid* SISLY, *her* COACHMAN,
                and THREE CARTERS

ANNE
  Bid my coach stay. Why should I ride in state,
  Being hurled so low down by the hand of fate?
  A seat like to my fortunes let me have,
  Earth for my chair, and for my bed a grave.

14 *run* Q1 (ran Q3)
14 *division* a melodic passage in music, a run, rapidly executed
16–17 *frets* a pun on the senses (a) divisions of the fingerboard of the lute, and (b)
  fretting sores, cankers
16 *pleasant* merry, jocular
19 *chance* fortune
21 *being well strung i.e.* presumably her voice
22 *strange* exceptional, wonderful
29 *bestead* situated, circumstanced

JENKIN
    Comfort, good mistress; you have watered your coach   5
    with tears already. You have but two mile now to go to
    your manor. A man cannot say by my old Master
    Frankford as he may say by me, that he wants manors, for
    he hath three or four, of which this is one that we are
    going to.   10

SISLY
    Good mistress, be of good cheer. Sorrow you see hurts
    you, but helps you not. We all mourn to see you so sad.

CARTER
    Mistress, I spy one of my landlord's men
    Come riding post. 'Tis like he brings some news.

ANNE
    Comes he from Master Frankford, he is welcome,   15
    So are his news, because they come from him.

                    Enter NICK

NICK
    There.   [*Gives her the lute*]
ANNE
    I know the lute. Oft have I sung to thee;
    We both are out of tune, both out of time.

NICK
    [*Aside*] Would that had been the worst instrument that 20
    e'er you played on. [*To her*] My master commends him to
    ye; there's all he can find that was ever yours. He hath
    nothing left that ever you could lay claim to, but his own
    heart, and he could afford you that. All that I have to
    deliver you is this. He prays you to forget him, and so he 25
    bids you farewell.

---

    8 *manors* a pun, of course, on 'manners'
    10 *to* Q1 (to now Q3)
    13 *spy one* Q1 (see some Q3)
    14 *post* in haste
    16 *are* Q1 (is Q3)
    19 *out of tune, both out of time i.e.* are both instruments of discord and disharmony
    20 *the worst instrument i.e.* with the implication of another, sexual instrument
    21 *to* Q1 (vnto Q3)
    23 *lay claim to* Q3 (claim to lay Q1)

---

    18 *I know the lute* Q1, Q3. The conjectured reading, 'I know thee, lute,' proposed by
    G.B. Johnston in *N.&Q.*, cciii (1958), pp. 525-6, should be mentioned. It is
    possible, but unnecessary

ANNE

    I thank him. He is kind and ever was.
    All you that have true feeling of my grief,
    That know my loss, and have relenting hearts,
    Gird me about, and help me with your tears   30
    To wash my spotted sins. My lute shall groan;
    It cannot weep, but shall lament my moan.

                                        [She plays]

Enter WENDOLL

WENDOLL

    Pursued with horror of a guilty soul,
    And with the sharp scourge of repentance lashed,
    I fly from my own shadow. O my stars!   35
    What have my parents in their lives deserved
    That you should lay this penance on their son?
    When I but think of Master Frankford's love,
    And lay it to my treason, or compare
    My murdering him for his relieving me,   40
    It strikes a terror like a lightning's flash
    To scorch my blood up. Thus I like the owl,
    Ashamed of day, live in these shadowy woods
    Afraid of every leaf or murmuring blast,
    Yet longing to receive some perfect knowledge   45
    How he hath dealt with her. *[Sees* ANNE*]* O my sad fate!
    Here, and so far from home, and thus attended!
    O God, I have divorced the truest turtles
    That ever lived together, and being divided
    In several places, make their several moan;   50
    She in the fields laments, and he at home.
    So poets write that Orpheus made the trees
    And stones to dance to his melodious harp,
    Meaning the rustic and the barbarous hinds,
    That had no understanding part in them;   55

30 *Gird me about* gather round me
33 WENDOLL Q1 (*omitted* Q3) See Note on the Text pp. xxx–xxxi
35 *my own* Q1 (mine owne Q3)
37 *their* Q1 (your Q3)
39 *lay it to i.e.* in comparison
45 *perfect* certain, reliable
48 *truest turtles* The fidelity of the turtle dove to its mate was proverbial. See *Tilley,* T.624
50 *several* separate
52 *Orpheus* Legendary Greek poet who could move even inanimate things by his music. Wendoll's interpretation of Orpheus' mythical power was familiar enough in the Renaissance
54 *hinds* rustics, boors

So she from these rude carters tears extracts,
Making their flinty hearts with grief to rise
And draw down rivers from their rocky eyes.

ANNE
   [*To* NICK] If you return unto your master say—
   Though not from me, for I am all unworthy   60
   To blast his name so with a strumpet's tongue—
   That you have seen me weep, wish myself dead—
   Nay, you may say too, for my vow is past,
   Last night you saw me eat and drink my last.
   This to your master you may say and swear,   65
   For it is writ in heaven and decreèd here.

NICK
   I'll say you wept; I'll swear you made me sad.
   Why, how now, eyes? What now? What's here to do?
   I am gone, or I shall straight turn baby too.

WENDOLL
   [*Aside*] I cannot weep; my heart is all on fire.   70
   Cursed be the fruits of my unchaste desire.

ANNE
   Go break this lute upon my coach's wheel,
   As the last music that I e'er shall make—
   Not as my husband's gift, but my farewell
   To all earth's joy; and so your master tell.   75

NICK
   If I can for crying.

WENDOLL [*Aside*]   Grief, have done,
   Or like a madman I shall frantic run.

ANNE
   You have beheld the woefullest wretch on earth,
   A woman made of tears. Would you had words
   To express but what you see; my inward grief   80
   No tongue can utter. Yet, unto your power
   You may describe my sorrow, and disclose
   To thy sad master my abundant woes.

58 *down* Q3 (*omitted* Q1)
59 *your* Q1 (*my* Q3)
61 *blast* wither
61 *so* Q3 (*omitted* Q1)
72 *upon* Q3 (*omitted* Q1)
81 *unto your power* as far as you are able

NICK
  I'll do your commendations.

ANNE   O no!
  I dare not so presume, nor to my children;   85
  I am disclaimed in both; alas, I am.
  O never teach them when they come to speak
  To name the name of mother. Chide their tongue
  If they by chance light on that hated word;
  Tell them 'tis naught, for when that word they name,   90
  Poor pretty souls, they harp on their own shame.

WENDOLL
  [*Aside*] To recompense her wrongs, what canst thou do?
  Thou hast made her husbandless and childless too.

ANNE
  I have no more to say. Speak not for me,
  Yet you may tell your master what you see.   95

NICK
  I'll do it.   *Exit* NICK

WENDOLL
  [*Aside*] I'll speak to her, and comfort her in grief.
  O, but her wound cannot be cured with words.
  No matter though, I'll do my best good will,
  To work a cure on her whom I did kill.   100

ANNE
  So, now unto my coach, then to my home,
  So to my deathbed, for from this sad hour
  I never will nor eat, nor drink, nor taste
  Of any cates that may preserve my life.
  I never will nor smile, nor sleep, nor rest,   105
  But when my tears have washed my black soul white,
  Sweet Saviour, to Thy hands I yield my sprite.

WENDOLL
  [*To her*] O Mistress Frankford!

ANNE   O for God's sake fly!
  The Devil doth come to tempt me ere I die.
  My coach! This sin that with an angel's face   110

84 *do your commendations* present your remembrances, greetings
90 *naught* presumably a pun (a) nothing (b) wicked, bad
90 *word* Q3 (wotd Q1)
104 *cates* victuals, food
107 *sprite* spirit

Courted mine honour till he sought my wrack,
In my repentant eyes seems ugly black.

Exeunt all [except WENDOLL *and* JENKIN],
the CARTERS *whistling*

JENKIN
What, my young master that fled in his shirt? How come
you by your clothes again? You have made our house in a
sweet pickle, have you not, think you? What, shall I serve   115
you still, or cleave to the old house?

WENDOLL
Hence, slave! Away with thy unseasoned mirth.
Unless thou canst shed tears, and sigh, and howl,
Curse thy sad fortunes, and exclaim on fate,
Thou art not for my turn.   120

JENKIN
Marry, and you will not, another will. Farewell and be
hanged. Would you had never come to have kept this coil
within our doors. We shall ha' you run away like a sprite
again.

[*Exit* JENKIN]

WENDOLL
She's gone to death; I live to want and woe,   125
Her life, her sins, and all upon my head.
And I must now go wander like a Cain
In foreign countries and remoted climes,
Where the report of my ingratitude
Cannot be heard. I'll over first to France,   130

111 *Courted* Q1 (Coniur'd Q3)
111 *wrack* ruin, downfall
112 *eyes* Q1 (eye Q3)
115 *have you* Q1 (ha'ye Q3)
117 *unseasoned* untimely, unseasonable
119 *exclaim on* blame, make an outcry against
120 *for my turn* suitable for my purposes or requirements
121 *Marry* Originally an oath invoking the Virgin Mary, here merely an interjection
121 *and* if
122 *coil* confusion, disturbance
123 *sprite* spirit, ghost
127 *Cain* Biblical character condemned to wander the earth in punishment for the
murder of his brother, Abel. See *Genesis* iv, 8-14
128 *remoted* remote

112 s.d. *the* CARTERS *whistling* Van Fossen observes that Carters were famous for their
whistling, but this hardly seems the appropriate moment for a tune. Perhaps they
are rather stirring their beasts to action again

And so to Germany, and Italy,
Where, when I have recovered, and by travel
Gotten those perfect tongues, and that these rumours
May in their height abate, I will return.
And I divine, however now dejected,   135
My worth and parts being by some great man praised,
At my return I may in court be raised.

                                       Exit WENDOLL

SCENE XVII

Enter SIR FRANCIS, SIR CHARLES, CRANWELL, MALBY *and* SUSAN

SIR FRANCIS
Brother, and now my wife, I think these troubles
Fall on my head by justice of the heavens,
For being so strict to you in your extremities,
But we are now atoned. I would my sister
Could with like happiness o'ercome her griefs,   5
As we have ours.

SUSAN
You tell us, Master Cranwell, wonderous things
Touching the patience of that gentleman.
With what strange virtue he demeans his grief.

CRANWELL
I told you what I was witness of.   10
It was my fortune to lodge there that night.

SIR FRANCIS
O that same villain Wendoll! 'Twas his tongue
That did corrupt her; she was of herself
Chaste and devoted well. Is this the house?

CRANWELL
Yes, sir, I take it here your sister lies.   15

SIR FRANCIS
My brother Frankford showed too mild a spirit
In the revenge of such a loathed crime.
Less than he did, no man of spirit could do.
I am so far from blaming his revenge
That I commend it. Had it been my case   20

133 *Gotten those perfect tongues* learned those languages perfectly
  4 *atoned* reconciled, set at one
  9 *demeans* manages, governs
 14 *devoted well* very faithful

Their souls at once had from their breasts been freed.
Death to such deeds of shame is the due meed.

Enter JENKIN *and* SISLY

JENKIN
O my mistress, my mistress, my poor mistress!

SISLY
Alas that ever I was born! What shall I do for my poor
mistress?   25

SIR CHARLES
Why, what of her?

JENKIN
O Lord, sir, she no sooner heard that her brother and his
friends were come to see how she did, but she for very
shame of her guilty conscience fell into a swoon, and we
had much ado to get life into her.   30

SUSAN
Alas that she should bear so hard a fate;
Pity it is repentance comes too late.

SIR FRANCIS
Is she so weak in body?

JENKIN
O sir, I can assure you there's no help of life in her, for she
will take no sustenance. She hath plainly starved   35
herself, and now she is as lean as a lath. She ever looks for
the good hour. Many gentlemen and gentlewomen of the
country are come to comfort her.

22 *meed* recompense, reward, desert
22 s.d. *and* SISLY Q1 (*omitted* Q3)
23 *my mistress* Q1 (mistris Q3)
27–30 *Lineation as prose* Q3 (*as verse* Q1)
27 *his* Q1 (hir Q3)
29 *a* Q1 (such a Q3)
29 *and* Q1 (that Q3)
30 *into* Q1 (in Q3)
34–8 *Lineation as prose* Q3 (*as verse* Q1)
34 *help* Q1 (hope Q3)
36 *and* Q3 (that Q1)
36 *lath* a thin narrow strip of wood

Enter ANNE *in her bed*

MALBY

How fare you, Mistress Frankford?

ANNE

Sick, sick, O sick! Give me some air, I pray you.   40
Tell me, O tell me, where's Master Frankford?
Will not he deign to see me ere I die?

MALBY

Yes, Mistress Frankford; divers gentlemen,
Your loving neighbours, with that just request
Have moved and told him of your weak estate,   45
Who, though with much ado to get belief,
Examining of the general circumstance,
Seeing your sorrow and your penitence,
And hearing therewithal the great desire
You have to see him ere you left the world,   50
He gave to us his faith to follow us,
And sure he will be here immediately.

ANNE

You half revived me with those pleasing news.
Raise me a little higher in my bed.
Blush I not, brother Acton? Blush I not, Sir Charles?   55
Can you not read my fault writ in my cheek?
Is not my crime there? Tell me, gentlemen.

SIR CHARLES

Alas, good mistress, sickness hath not left you
Blood in your face enough to make you blush.

---

37 *good hour i.e.* the hour of her death, when she will enter into the life hereafter
40 *pray you* Q1 (pray Q3)
42 *he* Q1 (*omitted* Q3)
46 *though with much ado to get belief i.e.* though these neighbours had great difficulty in getting Frankford to believe them
51 *faith* promise
53 *half* Q1 (haue half Q3)
53 *those* Q1 (the Q3)
55 *brother Acton* Q3 (maister Frankford Q1)

---

38 s.d. *Enter* ANNE *in her bed* Precisely how such an entrance was accomplished is not quite clear, but it was by no means uncommon in the drama of the period. The bed may have been carried onto the stage or thrust out, or it may have been that she was simply 'discovered' by the drawing aside of a curtain over an inner, recessed stage. The conventional flexibility of the Jacobean stage as regards location is well exemplified by this scene

ANNE
    Then sickness like a friend my fault would hide.   60
    Is my husband come? My soul but tarries
    His arrive and I am fit for heaven.

SIR FRANCIS
    I came to chide you, but my words of hate
    Are turned to pity and compassionate grief.
    I came to rate you, but my brawls, you see,   65
    Melt into tears, and I must weep by thee.
    Here's Master Frankford now.

Enter FRANKFORD

FRANKFORD
    Good morrow, brother; good morrow, gentlemen.
    God, that hath laid this cross upon our heads,
    Might, had He pleased, have made our cause of meeting   70
    On a more fair and a more contented ground.
    But He that made us, made us to this woe.

ANNE
    And is he come? Methinks that voice I know.

FRANKFORD
    How do you, woman?

ANNE
    Well, Master Frankford, well; but shall be better,   75
    I hope, within this hour. Will you vouchsafe,
    Out of your grace and your humanity,
    To take a spotted strumpet by the hand?

FRANKFORD
    That hand once held my heart in faster bonds
    Than now 'tis gripped by me. God pardon them   80
    That made us first break hold.

60 *Then ... hide.* Q3 (*line attributed to Sir Charles* Q1)
62 *and* Q1 (then Q3)
63-7 SIR FRANCIS Q3 (*speech attributed to Sir Charles* Q1)
65 *rate* berate, reproach
65 *brawls* scoldings, quarrellings
67 s.d. *Enter* FRANKFORD Q3 (*given before line 67 in* Q1)
68 *good morrow* Q1 (morrow Q3)
71 *and a* Q1 (and Q3)
71 *more contented ground i.e.* for happier reasons
72 *to this woe i.e.* that we might suffer this woe
75 *better i.e.* in heaven
78 *spotted* morally blemished
79 *That* Q1 (This Q3)

ANNE   Amen, amen.
  Out of my zeal to heaven, whither I am now bound,
  I was so impudent to wish you here,
  And once more beg your pardon. O good man
  And father to my children, pardon me.   85
  Pardon, O pardon me! My fault so heinous is
  That if you in this world forgive it not,
  Heaven will not clear it in the world to come.
  Faintness hath so usurped upon my knees
  That kneel I cannot; but on my heart's knees   90
  My prostrate soul lies thrown down at your feet
  To beg your gracious pardon. Pardon, O pardon me!

FRANKFORD
  As freely from the low depth of my soul
  As my Redeemer hath forgiven his death,
  I pardon thee. I will shed tears for thee,   95
  Pray with thee, and in mere pity
  Of thy weak state I'll wish to die with thee.

ALL
  So do we all.

NICK
  [Aside] So will not I!
  I'll sigh and sob, but, by my faith, not die.   100

SIR FRANCIS
  O Master Frankford, all the near alliance
  I lose by her shall be supplied in thee.
  You are my brother by the nearest way;
  Her kindred hath fallen off, but yours doth stay.

FRANKFORD
  Even as I hope for pardon at that day   105
  When the Great Judge of Heaven in scarlet sits,
  So be thou pardoned. Though thy rash offence
  Divorced our bodies, thy repentant tears
  Unite our souls.

---

89 *unsurped upon* taken possession of
93 *from the low depth of* i.e. from the bottom of
96–7 *Lineation* Q1 (Pray with thee . . . estate,/Ile wish . . . Q3)
96 *mere* complete, absolute
97 *state* Q1 (estate Q3)
101 *near alliance* close kinship
104 *Her kindred hath fallen off* i.e. because she is about to die, she will be no longer be my sister
106 *in scarlet* i.e. in the robes of office of a judge

SIR CHARLES   Then comfort, Mistress Frankford;
  You see your husband hath forgiven your fall;   110
  Then rouse your spirits and cheer your fainting soul.

SUSAN
  How is it with you?

SIR CHARLES   How do you feel yourself?

ANNE
  Not of this world.

FRANKFORD
  I see you are not, and I weep to see it.
  My wife, the mother to my pretty babes,   115
  Both those lost names I do restore thee back,
  And with this kiss I wed thee once again.
  Though thou art wounded in thy honoured name,
  And with that grief upon they deathbed liest,
  Honest in heart, upon my soul thou diest.   120

ANNE
  Pardoned on earth, soul, thou in heaven art free.
  Once more thy wife dies thus embracing thee.

                                          [ANNE *dies*]

FRANKFORD
  New married, and new widowed; O she's dead,
  And a cold grave must be our nuptial bed.

SIR CHARLES
  Sir, be of good comfort, and your heavy sorrow   125
  Part equally amongst us; storms divided
  Abate their force, and with less rage are guided.

CRANWELL
  Do, Master Frankford; he that hath least part
  Will find enough to drown one troubled heart.

SIR FRANCIS
  Peace be with thee, Nan. Brothers and gentlemen,   130
  All we that can plead interest in her grief,
  Bestow upon her body funeral tears.
  Brother, had you with threats and usage bad
  Punished her sin, the grief of her offence
  Had not with such true sorrow touched her heart.   135

---

112 *do you* Q1 (de'ye Q3)
118 *thy honoured name* your reputation
122 *Once more thy wife i.e.* having once more been restored to being your wife, (she
    dies...)

FRANKFORD

 I see it had not; therefore on her grave
 I will bestow this funeral epitaph,
 Which on her marble tomb shall be engraved.
 In golden letters shall these words be filled:
 Here lies she whom her husband's kindness killed. 140

THE EPILOGUE

An honest crew, disposed to be merry,
Came to a tavern by and called for wine.
The drawer brought it, smiling like a cherry,
And told them it was pleasant, neat, and fine.
   'Taste it,' quoth one. He did so. 'Fie!' quoth he,   5
   'This wine was good; now't runs too near the lee.'

Another sipped, to give the wine his due,
And said unto the rest it drunk too flat.
The third said it was old, the fourth too new.
'Nay,' quoth the fifth, 'the sharpness likes me not.'   10
   Thus, gentlemen, you see how in one hour
   The wine was new, old, flat, sharp, sweet, and sour.

Unto this wine we do allude our play,
Which some will judge too trivial, some too grave.
You, as our guests, we entertain this day   15
And bid you welcome to the best we have.
   Excuse us, then; good wine may be disgraced
   When every several mouth hath sundry taste.